Baking
Is
Fun

Volume 7

Recipe No. 514 - 593

Cover Recipe Page 20

ISBN 0-9691357-7-7

Printed and Bound in Canada

Introduction

Dear Reader:

Our seventh volume of Baking Is Fun includes many Classic European recipes. This book spans a broad area: from tortes to delicious savouries. It also includes some famous recipes such as, Sacher Torte, Dobos Torte, Lady Finger Torte and Battenburg Cake. Many of the recipes have new and innovative ways of presenting food to your friends and family. We hope that the 81 full colour photographs will encourage you to try some of these exciting recipes.

Additional copies may be obtained by writing to:

oetker Recipe Service
2229 Drew Road
Mississauga, Ontario
L5S 1E5

Contents

Tortes

Cherry Torte

Recipe No. 514

Batter:

4	egg yolks	4
15 mL	hot water	3 tbsp
100 g	sugar	1/2 cup
1 pkg	**oetker** vanilla sugar	1 pkg
1	egg white	1
60 g	all-purpose flour	1/2 cup
70 g	**oetker** Gustin corn starch	1/2 cup
5 mL	**oetker** baking powder	1 tsp

Almond Mixture:

3	egg whites	3
150 g	sugar	2/3 cup
1 pkg	**oetker** vanilla sugar	1 pkg
100 g	almonds, ground	1 cup

Buttercream:

1/2 pkg	**oetker** vanilla pudding	1/2 pkg
70 g	sugar	1/4 cup
250 mL	cold milk	1 cup
150 g	butter	2/3 cup
1 pkg	**oetker** vanilla sugar	1 pkg

Cherry Filling:

1/2 pkg	**oetker** vanilla pudding	1/2 pkg
15 mL	sugar	1 tbsp
250 mL	cold cherry juice	1 cup
400 g	sour cherries (stewed or canned), pitted, drained	1 3/4 cups

Soaking Mixture:

90 mL	water	6 tbsp
60 g	sugar	1/4 cup
90 mL	kirsch (cherry brandy)	6 tbsp

Decoration:

70 g	almonds, sliced, toasted	1/2 cup
30 g	icing sugar, sifted	1/4 cup

Sponge Batter:

PREHEAT oven to 175°C (350°F). Line a
25 cm (10") springform pan with waxed paper.
WHIP egg yolks and hot water until fluffy.
Gradually add two-thirds of the sugar and
vanilla sugar. Continue to beat until mixture is
creamy.
BEAT egg white to stiff peaks. Gradually add
remaining sugar. Spoon over creamed mixture.
MIX flour, corn starch and baking powder. Sift
over creamed mixture. Fold in gently but
thoroughly.
SPREAD batter evenly in prepared pan.
BAKE on lower oven rack for 25-30 minutes.
REMOVE from pan. Cool completely.

Almond Mixture:

PREHEAT oven to 150°C (300°F). Line the
bottom of a 25 cm (10") springform pan with
waxed paper (the sides will not be used).
BEAT egg whites to very stiff peaks.
COMBINE sugar and vanilla sugar. Fold
gently but thoroughly into egg white mixture
one spoonful at a time. Fold in ground
almonds.
SPREAD half of mixture over bottom of
prepared ringless pan.
BAKE on middle oven rack for 30-35 minutes,
until golden. Remove waxed paper
immediately.
BAKE remaining batter in the method outlined
above.

Buttercream:

PREPARE pudding (one-half pkg) according
to package directions using milk and sugar
quantities in Buttercream recipe. Let cool.
WHIP butter until fluffy. Add vanilla sugar.
Stir butter mixture into pudding one spoonful
at a time.

Cherry Filling:

PREPARE remaining pudding (one-half pkg)
according to package directions, substituting
cherry juice for milk. Fold in cherries, gently
but thoroughly. Let cool.

Soaking:

BOIL water and sugar. Let cool. Add kirsch.
SLICE cake once to make two layers.
DRIZZLE both layers of the cake on the cut
side with kirsch syrup.
SPREAD one-fifth of the buttercream mixture
evenly over one layer of baked almond mixture.
TOP with one layer of sponge cake.
FILL pastry bag fitted with a star tube with
one-fifth of buttercream mixture.
FORM three concentric circles on top of the
sponge cake.
FILL insides of circles with cherry filling.
TOP with second layer of sponge cake and
spread with one-fifth of buttercream mixture.
TOP with final layer of baked almond mixture.
SPREAD remaining buttercream mixture over
sides of cake. Cover sides with almonds.
SPRINKLE top of cake with icing sugar.

Fruit Torte

Recipe No. 515

Batter:

4	egg yolks	4	
100 g	sugar	½ cup	
1 pkg	**oetker** vanilla sugar	1 pkg	
4	egg whites	4	
150 g	all-purpose flour	1¼ cups	
2 mL	**oetker** baking powder	½ tsp	

Pudding:

½ pkg	**oetker** vanilla pudding	½ pkg	
250 mL	milk	1 cup	
20 g	sugar	1 tbsp	

Topping:

500-750 mL	fruit, fresh, stewed or canned (e.g. pineapple, peaches, strawberries, bananas, oranges)	2-3 cups	

Glaze:

1 pkg	**oetker** instant clear glaze	1 pkg	

Decoration:

125 mL	whipping cream	½ cup	
5 mL	**oetker** Whip it	1 tsp	
5 mL	sugar	1 tsp	
35 g	almonds, sliced	¼ cup	

Batter:

PREHEAT oven to 160°C (325°F). Grease a 25 cm (10") flan pan.

WHIP egg yolks until fluffy. Gradually add two-thirds of the sugar and vanilla sugar. Continue to beat until mixture is creamy.

BEAT the egg whites to stiff peaks. Gradually add the remaining sugar.

SPOON egg whites over creamed mixture.

COMBINE flour and baking powder. Sift over creamed mixture. Fold in gently but thoroughly.

SPREAD batter evenly in prepared pan.

BAKE on lower oven rack for 30-35 minutes.

REMOVE from pan. Cool completely.

Pudding:

PREPARE pudding (one-half package) according to package directions using milk and sugar quantities in pudding recipe. Pour into bowl.

COVER surface with plastic wrap and chill.

Topping:

SPREAD pudding mixture on cake.

TOP with drained fruit.

Glaze:

PREPARE glaze according to package directions.

SPOON over fruit. Chill until glaze sets.

Decoration:

COMBINE whipping cream, Whip it and sugar.

BEAT according to package directions.

DECORATE torte with whipped cream and sliced almonds.

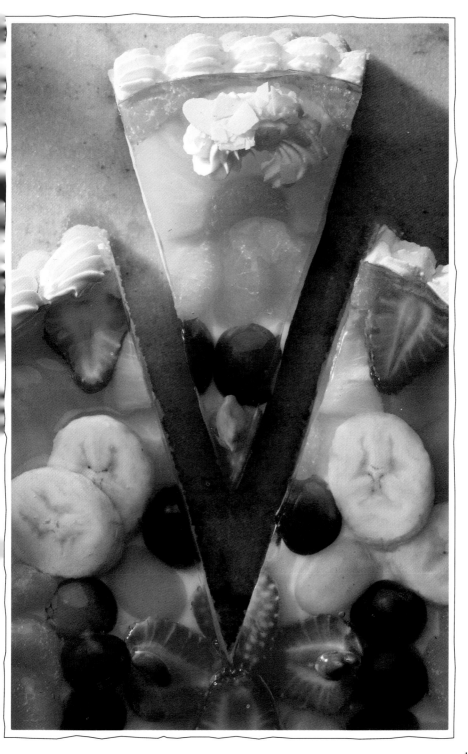

Glazed Nut Cake

Recipe No. 516

Batter:

6	eggs	6
250 g	sugar	1 cup
1 pkg	**oetker** vanilla sugar	1 pkg
150 g	walnuts, ground	1½ cups
250 g	all-purpose flour	2 cups
10 mL	**oetker** baking powder	2 tsp

Filling:

50 g	apricot jam	¼ cup
50 mL	rum	¼ cup

Brushing:

30 mL	hot apricot jam	2 tbsp

Lemon Glaze:

250 g	icing sugar, sifted	2½ cups
15 mL	lemon juice	1 tbsp
30 mL	water	2 tbsp

Batter:
PREHEAT oven to 175°C (350°F). Grease a 25 cm (10") springform pan.
WHIP eggs until fluffy. Gradually add sugar and vanilla sugar.
CONTINUE to beat until mixture is creamy. ADD the nuts.
MIX together flour and baking powder. Sift over the creamed mixture. Fold in gently but thoroughly.
SPREAD batter evenly in prepared pan.
BAKE on lower oven rack for 45-50 minutes.
REMOVE from pan. Cool completely.

Filling:
BRING the jam to a boil and add the rum.
SLICE the cake once to make two layers.
SPREAD one-half of the jam on bottom layer and top with second layer.

Brushing:
SPREAD sides and top of cake thinly with remaining jam.

Glaze:
COMBINE sifted icing sugar and lemon juice. ADD water until a thick paste is obtained. SPREAD over cake immediately.

Poppy Seed Torte

Recipe No. 517

Batter:

110 g	butter or margarine	½	cup
150 g	sugar	⅔	cup
1 pkg	**oetker** vanilla sugar	1	pkg
6	egg yolks	6	
150 g	poppy seeds	1	cup
70 g	almonds, ground	¾	cup
5 mL	**oetker** baking powder	1	tsp
5 mL	cinnamon	1	tsp
6	egg whites	6	

Filling:

60 mL	red currant jam	4	tbsp

Lemon Glaze:

250 g	icing sugar, sifted	2½	cups
15 mL	lemon juice	1	tbsp
30 mL	water	2	tbsp

Batter:

PREHEAT oven to 160°C (325°F). Line a 21 cm (8") springform pan with waxed paper.
WHIP the butter or margarine until fluffy. Gradually add sugar, vanilla sugar and egg yolks.
MIX poppy seeds, almonds, baking powder and cinnamon. Stir into butter mixture.
BEAT egg whites to stiff peaks. Fold into butter mixture gently but thoroughly.
SPREAD batter evenly in prepared pan.
BAKE on lower oven rack for 60-70 minutes.
REMOVE from pan. Cool completely.

Filling:

SLICE cake once to make two layers.
SPREAD 30 mL (two tablespoons) of the jam over the bottom layer. Cover with second layer.
SPREAD remaining jam on sides and top of cake.

Glaze:

COMBINE sifted icing sugar and lemon juice. Add water until a thick paste is obtained.
SPREAD over cake immediately.

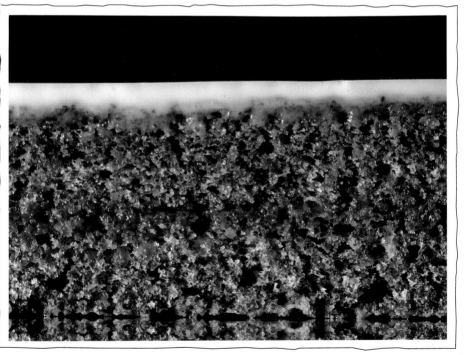

13

*S*acher Torte

Recipe No. 518

Batter:

200 g	butter, softened	³/₄	cup
140 g	icing sugar, sifted	1¹/₄	cups
8	egg yolks	8	
200 g	semi-sweet chocolate	7	squares
8	egg whites	8	
140 g	sugar	³/₄	cup
180 g	all-purpose flour	1¹/₃	cups

Filling:

150 g	apricot jam	¹/₂	cup

Brushing:

15 mL	hot apricot jam	1	tbsp

Chocolate Glaze:

100 g	semi-sweet chocolate	3¹/₂	squares
300 g	sugar	1¹/₃	cups
1 pkg	**oetker** vanilla sugar	1	pkg
125 mL	water	¹/₂	cup

Batter:
PREHEAT oven to 160°C (325°F). Line a
25 cm (10") springform pan with waxed paper.
WHIP butter and icing sugar until fluffy.
Gradually add egg yolks and stir until mixture
is creamy.
SOFTEN chocolate in a double boiler. Stir into
the creamed mixture one spoonful at a time.
BEAT egg whites to stiff peaks. Continue to
beat. Gradually add sugar.
SPOON the egg white mixture over the
creamed mixture.
SIFT the flour over the creamed mixture and
stir gently but thoroughly.
SPREAD batter evenly in prepared pan.
BAKE on lower oven rack for 55-60 minutes.
LET cool in pan for approximately five
minutes.
REMOVE from pan and turn onto wire cake
rack. Let cool completely.

Filling:
SLICE cake once to make two layers.
SPREAD bottom layer with apricot jam and
cover with top layer.

Brushing:
BEFORE glazing, brush cake thinly with jam.

Glaze:
BREAK chocolate into pieces and in a
saucepan, melt slowly.
IN another saucepan combine sugar, vanilla
sugar and water.
BOIL to a 'Strong Thread' 106°C (223°F). Let
cool to approximately 35°C (95°F).
ADD melted chocolate. With a mixing spoon
stir along edge of saucepan until a thin skin
forms on the surface.
GLAZE prepared cake.

Dobos Torte

Recipe No. 519

Batter:

6	eggs	6
170 g	sugar	3/4 cup
1 pkg	**oetker** vanilla sugar	1 pkg
150 g	all-purpose flour	1 1/4 cups
5 mL	**oetker** baking powder	1 tsp

Glazed Cake Slice:

210 g	icing sugar, sifted	1 3/4 cups
1	24 cm (9") purchased cake slice	1

Filling:

200 g	semi-sweet chocolate	7 squares
250 g	butter	1 cup
210 g	icing sugar, sifted	1 3/4 cups
30 g	cocoa, sifted	1/3 cup
1	egg yolk	1
1 btl	**oetker** rum flavouring concentrate	1 btl

Decoration:

50 g	semi-sweet chocolate, shaved	2 squares

Batter:
PREHEAT oven to 175°C (350°F). Line a 24 cm (9") springform pan with waxed paper.
WHIP eggs until fluffy. Gradually add sugar and vanilla sugar.
CONTINUE to beat until mixture is creamy.
MIX together flour and baking powder. Sift over creamed mixture.
STIR into mixture gently but thoroughly.
DIVIDE batter into five equal portions.
SPOON one-fifth of batter evenly into prepared pan.*
BAKE on lower oven rack for 10-15 minutes.
REMOVE from pan. Cool completely.
REPEAT * four times.

Glazed (Purchased) Cake Slice:
SIFT the icing sugar into a saucepan and heat until golden yellow, to form a glaze.
GREASE a knife and spread the glaze over the cake slice.
USING a greased knife, cut cake into twelve sections immediately.

Filling:
MELT the chocolate in a double-boiler on low heat. Stir until mixture is a smooth consistency. Let cool.
WHIP butter until fluffy. Gradually add sifted icing sugar, cocoa, egg yolk, flavouring concentrate, and cooled chocolate. Stir well.
SPREAD the individual cake layers with two-thirds of the filling and place together. (The top layer must be filling.)
FILL a pastry bag, fitted with a star tube, with remaining filling. (Set aside some filling for the sides of the cake.)
SECTION the cake into twelve portions without cutting it.
PIPE a filling spiral on each portion.

Decoration:
DECORATE the sides of the cake with filling. Sprinkle with shaved chocolate.
PLACE each of the previously glazed slices against each spiral so that it resembles a fan-like structure, as illustrated.

*T*ira-mi-su Cake

Recipe No. 520

Batter:

4	egg yolks	4
100 g	sugar	1/2 cup
1 pkg	**oetker** vanilla sugar	1 pkg
4	egg whites	4
150 g	all-purpose flour	1 1/4 cups
2 mL	**oetker** baking powder	1/2 tsp

Filling:

125 mL	red wine	1/2 cup
50 g	sugar	1/4 cup
	juice and grated peel of 1 lemon	
	grated peel of 2 oranges	
	juice of 3-4 oranges	
60 mL	rum	1/3 cup
300 g	lady fingers, crumbled	12 oz
100 g	semi-sweet chocolate, chopped	3 1/2 squares

Spreading:

	hot apricot or red currant jam	

Glaze:

200 g	icing sugar, sifted	1 1/2 cups
1	egg white	1
few drops	red food colouring	few drops

Batter:
PREHEAT oven to 175°C (350°F). Line a 24 cm (9") springform pan with waxed paper. WHIP eggs yolks until fluffy. Gradually add two-thirds of the sugar and vanilla sugar. Continue to beat until mixture is creamy. BEAT the egg whites to stiff peaks. Continue beating. Gradually add the remaining sugar. SPOON the egg whites over the creamed mixture. MIX together flour and baking powder. Sift over creamed mixture. Fold in gently but thoroughly. SPREAD batter evenly in prepared pan. BAKE on lower oven rack for 35-40 minutes. REMOVE from pan. Let cool.

Filling:
COMBINE wine, sugar, juice and grated peel of lemon and oranges in a saucepan. Bring to a boil. Let cool slightly. ADD rum, crumbled lady fingers and chocolate to the liquid. Stir. SLICE cake once to make two layers. PLACE bottom cake layer into a springform pan, without the base. SPREAD filling evenly over cake layer. Cover with second layer. COVER and press cake with the base of the springform pan. Weigh down. Let stand for one to two hours.

Spreading:
REMOVE cake from pan and spread with strained jam.

Glaze:
Mix together icing sugar, and egg white to obtain a thick consistency. Colour with a few drops of red food colouring. SPREAD evenly over cake.

Linzer Torte

Recipe No. 521

Batter:

150 g	all-purpose flour	1¼	cups
5 mL	**oetker** baking powder	1	tsp
210 g	icing sugar, sifted	1¾	cups
3	egg yolks	3	
15 mL	white wine	1	tbsp
250 g	cold butter	1	cup
100 g	breadcrumbs, toasted	½	cup
300 g	almonds, ground	3	cups
	grated peel of one lemon		
2 mL	cinnamon	½	tsp

Filling:

180 mL	red currant jam	¾	cup

For Brushing:

1	egg yolk, whipped	1	

Decoration:

30 g	almonds, sliced	¼	cup

Dough:
GREASE a 26 cm (10") springform pan with the ring removed.
MIX together flour and baking powder. Sift onto a working surface.
MAKE a well in the centre. Add icing sugar, egg yolks and wine. Add some flour and work into a thick paste.
CUT cold butter into small pieces over mixture. Add bread crumbs, almonds, grated lemon peel and cinnamon.
WORK all ingredients together into a smooth dough. Cover and chill for one-half hour.
PREHEAT oven to 180°C (350°F).
PLACE two-thirds of the dough on the bottom of a springform pan. Roll out evenly to cover. Put springform pan ring back into position. Prick dough with fork several times.

Filling:
SPREAD evenly with jam.
SHAPE some of the remaining dough into strips. Place in a lattice design over jam. Press remainder of dough around inside rim of the pan to form sides.

Brushing and Decorating:
BRUSH evenly with egg yolk. Sprinkle with almond slices.
BAKE on lower oven rack for 45-50 minutes.
REMOVE from pan and let cool.

Chestnut Cream Torte

Recipe No. 522

Batter:

4	eggs	4
150 g	sugar	²/₃ cup
1 pkg	**oetker** vanilla sugar	1 pkg
135 g	all-purpose flour	1 cup
2 mL	**oetker** baking powder	¹/₂ tsp
40 g	butter, melted	¹/₄ cup

Marron Cream:

375 g	chestnuts, shelled, cooked, grated	14 oz
250 mL	milk	1 cup
150 g	icing sugar, sifted	1¹/₃ cups
1 pkg	**oetker** vanilla sugar	1 pkg
30 mL	rum	2 tbsp
250 mL	whipping cream	1 cup

Decoration:

12-16	marrons glacès (made from 45 mL/3 tbsp of marron cream)	12 -16
1 pkg	**oetker** Chocofix	1 pkg
30 mL	chestnuts, cooked, grated	2 tbsp

Batter:

PREHEAT oven to 175°C (350°F). Line a 20 cm (8") springform pan with waxed paper.
WHIP the eggs until fluffy. Gradually add the sugar and vanilla sugar. Continue to beat until mixture is creamy.
SIFT together flour and baking powder. Spoon over creamed mixture. Fold in gently but thoroughly.
GRADUALLY add the cooled butter.
SPREAD batter evenly in prepared pan.
BAKE on lower oven rack for 30-35 minutes.
REMOVE from pan. Let cool.

Marron Cream:

COMBINE grated chestnuts and milk.
ADD icing sugar, vanilla sugar and rum. Stir until smooth.
BEAT whipping cream to stiff peaks. Gently fold into rum mixture.
SLICE cake twice to make three layers.
SET aside 45 mL (3 tbsp) of the marron cream.
SPREAD one-quarter of the marron cream over bottom layer and cover with second layer.
SPREAD one-half of the remaining cream on second layer and top with final layer.
SPREAD sides and top of cake evenly with remaining cream.

Decoration:

FILL a pastry bag, fitted with a star tube, with the reserved marron cream. On a sheet of aluminum foil pipe some marrons. Freeze for one hour.

Glaze:

PREPARE Chocofix according to package directions.
WITH the aid of toothpicks, dip each marron into the glaze.
LET set.
DECORATE the top of the cake with the marrons glacès and sprinkle with grated chestnuts.

Lady Finger Torte

Recipe No. 523

COMBINE water, orange and lemon juice in a saucepan. Bring to a boil. Gradually add sugar and rum. Let cool.

SOAK each lady finger individually in liquid mixture.

COVER the base of a 23 cm (9") springform pan with some of the lady fingers.

SPRINKLE with some of the ground hazelnuts.

Ingredients:

125	mL	water	¹/₂ cup	
		juice of 1 orange		
		juice of ¹/₂ lemon		
100	g	sugar	¹/₂ cup	
125	mL	rum	¹/₂ cup	
70-80		lady fingers	70-80	

For Sprinkling:

hazelnuts, ground

Filling:

1	pkg	**oetker** vanilla pudding	1	pkg
500	mL	milk	2	cups
45	mL	cherry liqueur	3	tbsp
1	btl	**oetker** rum flavouring concentrate	1	btl
150	g	butter	³/₄ cup	
50	g	hazelnuts, ground	¹/₂ cup	

Decoration:

250	mL	whipping cream	1	cup
5	mL	sugar	1	tsp
1	pkg	**oetker** vanilla sugar	1	pkg
1	pkg	**oetker** Whip it	1	pkg
A few		lady fingers	A few	

Filling:

PREPARE vanilla pudding according to package directions.

STIR in cherry liqueur and flavouring concentrate.

WHIP butter until fluffy. Fold into cooled (room temperature) pudding mixture one spoonful at a time. Stir in ground hazelnuts.

PLACE lady fingers and cream alternately in layers into pan. The top layer must consist of lady fingers.

COVER the torte with aluminum foil. Chill for three to four hours.

REMOVE the pan ring. Place the torte on a cake plate.

Decoration:

PUT whipping cream in a bowl.

ADD sugar, vanilla sugar and Whip it. Beat until peaks form.

PLACE mixture in a pastry bag fitted with a star tube.

DECORATE the torte with the whipped cream and lady fingers.

Black Forest Cherry Torte

Batter:

6	egg yolks	6	
180 g	sugar	³/₄	cup
1 pkg	**oetker** vanilla sugar	1	pkg
30 mL	hot water	2	tbsp
1 btl	**oetker** rum flavouring concentrate	1	btl
6	egg whites	6	
65 g	all-purpose flour	¹/₂	cup
20 g	cocoa	¹/₄	cup
45 mL	**oetker** Gustin corn starch	3	tbsp
5 mL	**oetker** baking powder	1	tsp

Sprinkling:

65 mL	kirsch (cherry brandy)	¹/₄	cup

Filling:

375 mL	cherry pie filling	1¹/₂	cups
500 mL	whipping cream	2	cups
2 pkgs	**oetker** Whip it	2	pkgs

Decoration:

50 g	semi-sweet chocolate, shaved	2	squares
	some maraschino cherries		

Batter:
PREHEAT oven to 180°C (350°F). Grease a 23 cm (9") springform pan.
COMBINE egg yolks, two-thirds of the sugar, vanilla sugar, hot water and flavouring concentrate in a mixing bowl.
BEAT at high speed until thick and creamy.
BEAT egg whites and remaining sugar to stiff peaks.
SIFT together flour, cocoa, corn starch, and baking powder.
FOLD into egg yolk mixture gently but thoroughly.
FOLD egg whites into egg yolk mixture gently.
TURN batter into prepared pan.
BAKE on middle oven rack for 35-40 minutes.
REMOVE from pan. Let cool completely.

Filling:
SLICE the cake twice to make three layers.
SPRINKLE the bottom layer with kirsch and cover with pie filling.
COMBINE whipping cream with Whip it and beat to stiff peaks.
SPREAD one-quarter of whipped cream over pie filling. Cover with second layer. Press tightly and sprinkle with kirsch.
SPREAD one-half of remaining whipped cream on second layer. Cover with final layer.
SET aside 60 mL (4 tbsp) of whipped cream for decoration.

Decoration:
SPREAD sides and top of cake with remaining whipped cream.
SPRINKLE the top of the cake with shaved chocolate.
DECORATE with reserved whipped cream and maraschino cherries.

Wine Cream Torte

Recipe No. 525

Sponge Batter:

3	egg yolks	3
45 mL	hot water	3 tbsp
150 g	sugar	³/₄ cup
1 pkg	**oetker** vanilla sugar	1 pkg
3	egg whites	3
90 g	all-purpose flour	²/₃ cup
100 g	**oetker** Gustin corn starch	³/₄ cup
15 mL	**oetker** baking powder	1 tbsp

Wine Cream:

1 pkg	**oetker** vanilla pudding	1 pkg
100 g	sugar	¹/₂ cup
375 mL	white wine	1¹/₂ cups
125 mL	whipping cream	¹/₂ cup

Decoration:

100 g	almonds, sliced	³/₄ cup
some	grapes	some

Batter:
PREHEAT oven to 175°C (350°F). Line a 24 cm (9¹/₂") springform pan with waxed paper.
WHIP egg yolks and hot water until fluffy. Gradually add two-thirds of the sugar and vanilla sugar. Continue to beat until mixture is creamy.
BEAT the egg whites to stiff peaks. Gradually beat in remaining sugar.
SPOON egg whites over creamed mixture.
SIFT together flour, corn starch and baking powder. Spoon over creamed mixture. Fold in gently but thoroughly.
POUR mixture into prepared pan.
BAKE on lower oven rack for 35-40 minutes.
REMOVE from pan and let cool.

Cream:
COMBINE vanilla pudding with sugar and 125 mL (¹/₂ cup) of the measured wine. Stir until smooth.
HEAT the remaining wine. Remove from heat.
ADD the pudding mixture. Quickly bring to a boil. Remove from heat.
POUR mixture into a bowl and chill. To prevent skin from forming, cover with plastic wrap.
BEAT whipping cream to stiff peaks. Gently but thoroughly fold into the chilled pudding mixture.
SLICE cake twice to make three layers.
SPREAD the bottom layer with one-third of the cream. Cover with second layer.
SPREAD second layer with one half of the remaining cream. Cover with final layer.
SPREAD sides and top of cake with cream (set aside 30 mL/2 tbsp). Sprinkle with almond slices.
DECORATE with reserved cream and grapes.

Truffle Bombe

Recipe No. 526

Batter:

50 g	butter	¹/₄	cup
60 g	icing sugar, sifted	¹/₂	cup
1 pkg	**oetker** vanilla sugar	1	pkg
2	egg yolks	2	
100 g	all-purpose flour, sifted	³/₄	cup
5 mL	**oetker** baking powder	1	tsp
15 mL	cocoa	1	tbsp
60 mL	milk	¹/₄	cup
2	egg whites	2	

Truffle Cream:

1	egg	1	
150 g	sugar	³/₄	cup
1 pkg	**oetker** vanilla sugar	1	pkg
30 mL	rum	2	tbsp
15 mL	cocoa	1	tbsp
50 g	nuts, ground	¹/₂	cup
50 g	chocolate, melted	¹/₃	cup
60 mL	whipping cream	¹/₄	cup
200 g	shortening, room temperature	1	cup

Glaze:

100 g	semi-sweet chocolate	4	squares
60 mL	whipping cream	¹/₄	cup

Batter:
PREHEAT oven to 180°C (350°F). Line a 20 cm (8") springform pan with waxed paper.
WHIP butter until fluffy. Gradually add icing sugar, vanilla sugar and egg yolks.
MIX together flour, baking powder and cocoa. Stir alternately with the milk into the butter mixture.
BEAT the egg whites to stiff peaks. Fold in gently but thoroughly.
SPREAD the batter evenly in prepared pan.
BAKE on lower oven rack for 30-35 minutes.
REMOVE from pan. Let cool completely.

Truffle Cream:
WHIP egg, sugar, vanilla sugar, rum and cocoa until fluffy.
STIR in nuts, chocolate and whipping cream.
ADD shortening. Stir mixture well and chill overnight.
SPREAD cream over cake so it forms a dome.

Glaze:
BREAK the chocolate into small pieces and place in a saucepan.
ADD whipping cream.
STIRRING constantly, bring to a boil. Let cool.
GLAZE prepared cake.

31

Quark Layer Cake

Recipe No. 527

Sponge Batter:

4	egg yolks	4
120 g	sugar	¹/₂ cup
1 pkg	**oetker** vanilla sugar	1 pkg
1 drop	**oetker** lemon flavouring concentrate	1 drop
4	egg whites	4
80 g	all-purpose flour	²/₃ cup

Filling:

500 mL	milk	2 cups
4	egg yolks	4
180 g	sugar	³/₄ cup
2 pkgs	**oetker** natural vanilla sugar	2 pkgs
3 drops	**oetker** lemon flavouring concentrate	3 drops
pinch	salt	pinch
2 pkgs	**oetker** gelatin powder	2 pkgs
500 g	quark	2 cups
	juice from ¹/₂ lemon	
500 mL	whipping cream	2 cups

Decoration:

30 g	icing sugar, sifted	¹/₄ cup

Optional Short-Cake Base

Batter:

150 g	all-purpose flour	1 cup
pinch	**oetker** baking powder	pinch
60 g	icing sugar, sifted	¹/₂ cup
¹/₂ pkg	**oetker** vanilla sugar	¹/₂ pkg
1 drop	**oetker** lemon flavouring concentrate	1 drop
110 g	cold butter or margarine	¹/₂ cup

Spreading:

45 mL	apricot jam	3 tbsp

Decoration:

30 g	icing sugar	¹/₄ cup

Batter:

PREHEAT oven to 180°C (350°F). Line a 25 cm (10") springform pan with waxed paper.
WHIP the egg yolks, two-thirds of the sugar, vanilla sugar and flavouring concentrate until fluffy.
BEAT the egg whites to stiff peaks. Gradually beat in remaining sugar.
SPOON the egg whites over the egg yolk mixture.
SIFT the flour over the egg whites. Fold in gently but thoroughly.
SPREAD batter evenly in prepared pan.
BAKE on lower oven rack for approximately 20 minutes.
REMOVE from pan. Let cool completely.

Filling:

SLICE the cake once to make two layers.
PLACE one layer into the springform pan.
COMBINE milk, egg yolks, sugar, vanilla sugar, flavouring concentrate, salt and gelatin in a saucepan.
HEAT, stirring constantly until gelatin has dissolved. Let cool.
STIR in quark and lemon juice.
BEAT whipping cream to stiff peaks. When the quark mixture begins to set, fold in whipped cream gently but thoroughly.
SPREAD entire mixture over cake layer in pan and cover with second layer. Chill the cake in the refrigerator for approximately three hours. After it has chilled completely, sprinkle with icing sugar.

Batter: (optional Short-Cake Base)

PREHEAT oven to 200°C (400°F).
COMBINE ingredients as listed and work into a smooth dough.
COVER with a cloth and let rest in a cool place for one-half hour.
PLACE dough on bottom of a ringless springform pan. Roll out evenly to cover. Put ring back into position.
BAKE on middle oven rack for 10-15 minutes.
REMOVE from pan. Let cool completely.
SPREAD short-cake base with apricot jam.
Cover with one layer of sponge cake. Place into springform pan.
SPREAD entire filling over cake and cover with final layer of sponge cake. Chill.
SPRINKLE with icing sugar.

Chocolate Cream Torte

Recipe No. 528

Batter:

5	egg yolks	5	
100 g	sugar	1/2	cup
1 pkg	**oetker** vanilla sugar	1	pkg
4	egg whites	4	
120 g	all-purpose flour	3/4	cup
5 mL	**oetker** baking powder	1	tsp
20 g	cocoa	1/4	cup

Filling:

1 pkg	**oetker** white chocolate mousse	1	pkg
170 mL	milk	3/4	cup

Decoration:

50 g	semi-sweet chocolate, shaved	2	squares

Batter:

PREHEAT oven to 180°C (350°F). Line a 23 cm (9") springform pan with waxed paper.
WHIP the egg yolks until fluffy. Gradually add two-thirds of the sugar and vanilla sugar. Continue to beat until mixture is creamy.
BEAT the egg whites to stiff peaks. Gradually beat in remaining sugar.
SPOON egg whites over creamed mixture.
MIX together flour, baking powder and cocoa. Sift over egg whites. Fold in gently but thoroughly.
SPREAD batter evenly in prepared pan.
BAKE on lower oven rack for 35-40 minutes.
REMOVE from pan and let cool.

Filling:

PREPARE the mousse according to package directions using 170 mL (3/4 cup) of cold milk.
CHILL.
SLICE the cake twice to make three layers.
FILL two layers with two-thirds of the mousse. Cover with final layer.
SPREAD sides and top of cake with remaining mousse.
SPRINKLE with shaved chocolate.

Hazelnut Torte

Recipe No. 529

Batter:

5	egg yolks	5
100 g	sugar	1/2 cup
1 pkg	**oetker** vanilla sugar	1 pkg
5	egg whites	5
200 g	hazelnuts, ground	2 1/4 cups
5 mL	**oetker** baking powder	1 tsp

Coffee Cream:

1 pkg	**oetker** vanilla pudding	1 pkg
375 mL	milk	1 1/2 cups
125 mL	strong coffee, cooled	1/2 cup
225 g	butter, room temperature	1 cup
150 g	sugar	1/4 cup

Decoration:

70 g	almond slices, toasted	3/4 cup
some	hazelnuts or halved walnuts	some

Batter:
PREHEAT oven to 175°C (350°F). Line a
20 cm (8") springform pan with waxed paper.
WHIP egg yolks until fluffy. Gradually add
sugar and vanilla sugar, beating until creamy.
BEAT egg whites to stiff peaks. Spoon over
creamed mixture.
MIX together hazelnuts and baking powder.
Fold into creamed mixture gently.
SPREAD batter evenly in prepared pan.
BAKE on lower oven rack for 50-60 minutes.
REMOVE from pan and let cool.

Coffee Cream:
DISSOLVE vanilla pudding in milk. Add
coffee. In a saucepan, over medium heat, bring
mixture to a boil. Reduce heat, stirring until
smoothly thickened. Pour into a bowl. Cover
with plastic wrap. Chill.
WHIP butter and sugar until fluffy. Add cooled
pudding mixture one spoonful at a time.
SLICE the cake twice. Spread two layers with
two-thirds of the cream. Place the third layer
on top.
SPREAD sides and top of cake evenly with
cream. Sprinkle almond slices on sides of cake.
Decorate top with remaining cream and nuts.

Cakes, Slices

Jelly Rolls

Doughnuts

Dough:

500 g	all-purpose flour	3¹/₂	cups
1 pkg	**oetker** instant dry yeast	1	pkg
pinch	salt		pinch
80 g	sugar	¹/₃	cup
1 pkg	**oetker** vanilla sugar	1	pkg
¹/₂ btl	**oetker** lemon flavouring concentrate	¹/₂	btl
45 mL	rum	3	tbsp
4	egg yolks	4	
80 g	butter, melted	¹/₃	cup
250 mL	lukewarm milk	1	cup

Filling:

150 mL	apricot jam	²/₃	cup

Deep Frying:

vegetable oil

Decoration:

40 g	icing sugar, sifted	¹/₃	cup
1 pkg	**oetker** vanilla sugar	1	pkg

Batter:

SIFT the flour into a mixing bowl, add yeast and mix well.

MAKE a well in the centre. Add salt, sugar, vanilla sugar, flavouring concentrate, rum, egg yolks, butter and milk.

KNEAD with an electric mixer fitted with dough hooks on high speed until dough is smooth, blistery and no longer sticky.

COVER with a cloth and let rest in a warm place until dough has doubled in size.

KNEAD the risen dough again briefly. Roll out evenly (about ¹/₂ cm / ³/₁₆" thick) onto a floured working surface.

CUT into circles with a cookie cutter.

PLACE a little jam in the centre of half of the circles. Top with remaining circles. Press edges together.

PLACE the doughnuts on a floured baking sheet. Cover with a cloth and let rest in a warm place until doubled in size.

FILL a deep fryer half way with vegetable oil. Heat slowly. (During the frying process the temperature should be kept at a constant, 180°C/350°F).

PLACE the doughnuts into the hot oil and cook for approximately one minute until the doughnuts are a golden brown. Turn doughnuts over and finish frying.

PLACE the doughnuts on paper towels to drain. Let cool on a wire rack.

MIX together icing sugar and vanilla sugar. Sprinkle on doughnuts.

Quick Tip

KNEAD the risen dough briefly.

SHAPE into a roll. Cut into 40 g pieces.

SHAPE the pieces into seamless balls. Place on a floured baking sheet and flatten slightly. Squeeze some jam into the centres using a pastry bag.

COVER with a cloth and let rest in a warm place until double in size.

FRY as directed above.

*F*ine Yeast Bundt Cake

Recipe No. 531

Batter:

500 g	all-purpose flour	3¹/₂ cups	
1 pkg	**oetker** instant dry yeast	1 pkg	
5 mL	salt	1 tsp	
70 g	sugar	¹/₄ cup	
1 pkg	**oetker** vanilla sugar	1 pkg	
45 mL	rum	3 tbsp	
	grated peel of a lemon		
1	egg	1	
5	egg yolks	5	
110 g	butter, melted	¹/₂ cup	
200 mL	lukewarm milk	³/₄ cup	
250 g	raisins	1¹/₂ cups	
50 g	almonds, ground	¹/₂ cup	

Decoration:

1 pkg	**oetker** vanilla sugar	1 pkg	

Batter:

GREASE a Bundt cake pan. Sprinkle bottom of pan with flour or ground nuts.

SIFT flour into a mixing bowl. Add yeast and mix well.

MAKE a well in the centre. Add salt, sugar, vanilla sugar, rum, lemon peel, egg, egg yolks, butter and milk.

KNEAD with an electric mixer fitted with dough hooks on high speed until dough is smooth, blistery and no longer sticky.

COVER with a cloth and let rest in a warm place until doubled in size.

KNEAD in raisins and almonds.

SPREAD dough evenly in prepared pan.

COVER with a cloth and let rest in a warm place until risen to three-quarters of its size.

PREHEAT oven to 180°C (350°F). Bake in preheated oven on lower oven rack for 45-50 minutes.

REMOVE from pan. Turn onto a wire cake rack. Let cool completely.

DECORATE by sprinkling with vanilla sugar.

Marble Cake

Recipe No. 532

Light Batter:

225	g	butter or margarine	1 cup
200	g	sugar	1 cup
1	pkg	**oetker** vanilla sugar	1 pkg
4		eggs	4
15	mL	rum	1 tbsp
400	g	all-purpose flour	3 cups
1	pkg	**oetker** baking powder	1 pkg
170	mL	milk	³/₄ cup

Dark Batter:

20	g	cocoa	¹/₄ cup
25	mL	icing sugar	1¹/₂ tbsp
30	mL	lukewarm milk	2 tbsp

Light Batter:

PREHEAT oven to 180°C (350°F). Grease a
1.5 L loaf pan or a Bundt cake pan. Sprinkle
bottom of pan with some breadcrumbs or flour.
WHIP the butter or margarine until fluffy.
Gradually add sugar, vanilla sugar, eggs and
rum.
SIFT together flour and baking powder.
STIR into butter mixture alternately with milk.
Add only enough milk until the batter drops
heavily from the spoon.
SPREAD two-thirds of the batter evenly in
prepared pan.

Dark Batter:

SIFT cocoa and icing sugar. Stir into the
remaining one-third light batter alternately
with milk. Again add only enough milk until the
batter drops heavily from the spoon.
SPREAD the dark batter over the light batter
in pan. Work a fork in a spiral fashion through
the dark and light batters to marble both
layers.
BAKE on lower oven rack for 50-60 minutes.
REMOVE from pan. Let cool completely.

Salzburger Bundt Cake

Recipe No. 533

Batter:

250 g	butter	1	cup
200 g	sugar	1	cup
1 pkg	**oetker** vanilla sugar	1	pkg
4	egg yolks	4	
1 btl	**oetker** rum flavouring concentrate	1	btl
pinch	salt		pinch
500 g	all-purpose flour	3¹/₂	cups
1 pkg	**oetker** baking powder	1	pkg
250 mL	milk	1	cup

Glaze:

210 g	icing sugar, sifted	1³/₄	cups
30 mL	hot water	2	tbsp

Decoration:

glacé cherries

Batter:

PREHEAT oven to 180°C (350°F). Grease a Bundt cake form.
WHIP the butter until fluffy. Gradually add sugar, vanilla sugar, egg yolks, flavouring concentrate and salt.
SIFT together flour and baking powder. Stir into butter mixture alternately with milk. Add only enough milk until the batter drops heavily from the spoon.
SPREAD batter evenly in prepared pan.
BAKE on lower oven rack for 55-60 minutes.
REMOVE from pan. Let cool completely.

Glaze:

COMBINE icing sugar with hot water. Stir until a thick paste consistency is reached.
SPREAD over entire cake.
DECORATE with cherries while glaze is still hot.

Raisin Bundt Cake

Recipe No. 534

Batter:

225 g	butter	1	cup
200 g	sugar	1	cup
1 pkg	**oetker** vanilla sugar	1	pkg
4	eggs	4	
6 drops	**oetker** lemon flavouring concentrate	6	drops
pinch	salt		pinch
500 g	all-purpose flour	3¹/₂	cups
1 pkg	**oetker** baking powder	1	pkg
125 mL	milk	¹/₂	cup
115 g	raisins	²/₃	cup
100 g	currants	²/₃	cup

Batter:

PREHEAT oven to 180°C (350°F). Grease a Bundt cake form.
WHIP butter until fluffy. Gradually add sugar, vanilla sugar, eggs, flavouring concentrate and salt.
SIFT together flour and baking powder.
STIR into butter mixture alternately with milk. Add only enough milk until the batter drops heavily from the spoon.
FOLD raisins and currants carefully into butter mixture.
SPREAD batter evenly in prepared pan.
BAKE on lower oven rack for 65-70 minutes.
REMOVE from pan. Let cool completely.

Rum Wreath

Recipe No. 535

Batter:

110 g	butter or margarine	½	cup
150 g	sugar	⅔	cup
3	eggs	3	
1 btl	**oetker** rum flavouring concentrate	1	btl
pinch	salt		pinch
150 g	all-purpose flour	1	cup
50 g	**oetker** Gustin corn starch	⅓	cup
10 mL	**oetker** baking powder	2	tsp

Soaking mixture:

90 mL	water	6	tbsp
50 g	sugar	¼	cup
90 mL	rum	6	tbsp

Filling and Decoration:

250 mL	whipping cream	1	cup
10 mL	sugar	2	tsp
1 pkg	**oetker** Whip it	1	pkg
45 mL	apricot jam, red jelly, for drizzling	3	tbsp

Batter:
PREHEAT oven to 160°C (325°F). Grease a ringform pan.
WHIP the butter or margarine until fluffy. Gradually add sugar, eggs, flavouring concentrate and salt.
SIFT together flour, corn starch and baking powder.
STIR into butter mixture gently but thoroughly one spoonful at a time.
SPREAD batter evenly in prepared pan.
BAKE on lower oven rack for 40-45 minutes.
REMOVE from pan and turn onto a wire cake rack. Let cool completely.
SLICE cake once to make two layers.

Soaking Mixture:
COMBINE water and sugar in a saucepan. Bring to a boil. Let cool.
ADD rum.
SOAK both layers, on the cut side, with the rum mixture.

Filling:
COMBINE whipping cream, sugar and Whip it.
BEAT to stiff peaks.
SPREAD the bottom cake layer with apricot jam and cover with one-third of the whipped cream. Cover wth second layer.
SPREAD top and sides with remaining cream.
DRIZZLE with jelly.

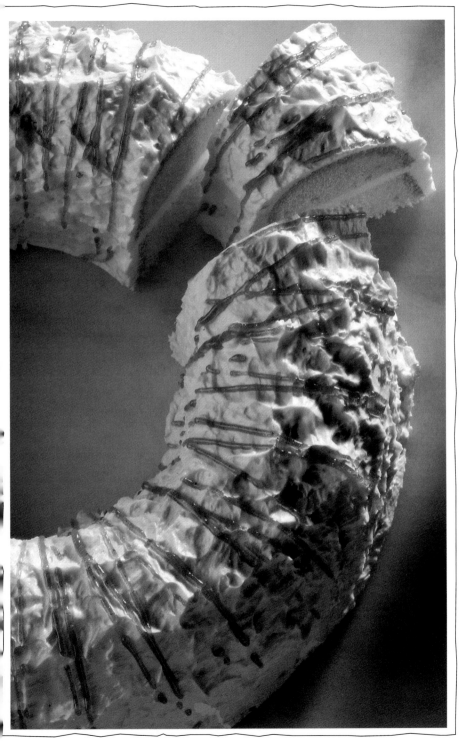

*S*pice Cake

Recipe No. 536

Batter:

150	g	butter or margarine	³/₄ cup
210	g	sugar	1 cup
1	pkg	**oetker** vanilla sugar	1 pkg
4		eggs	4
30	mL	rum	2 tbsp
pinch		each of ground nutmeg, cloves, coriander, cinnamon, aniseed	pinch
1	pkg	**oetker** baking powder	1 pkg
335	g	all-purpose flour	2¹/₂ cups
125	mL	milk	¹/₂ cup
125	g	raisins	³/₄ cup
100	g	walnuts, coarsely chopped	1 cup
100	g	semi-sweet chocolate, chopped	1 cup

Batter:

PREHEAT oven to 180°C (350°F). Grease a loaf pan. Sprinkle pan with flour or breadcrumbs.

WHIP butter or margarine until fluffy. Gradually add sugar, vanilla sugar, eggs, rum and spices.

SIFT together baking powder and flour. Stir into butter mixture alternately with milk. Add only enough milk until the batter drops heavily from the spoon.

FOLD in raisins, nuts and chocolate gently but thoroughly.

SPREAD batter evenly in prepared pan.

BAKE on lower oven rack for 65-70 minutes.

REMOVE from pan. Let cool.

Chocolate Fruit Cake

Recipe No. 537

Batter:

150 g	butter or margarine	³/₄	cup
150 g	sugar	²/₃	cup
1 pkg	**oetker** vanilla sugar	1	pkg
4	egg yolks	4	
150 g	semi-sweet chocolate, softened	6	squares
30 mL	rum	2	tbsp
2 mL	**oetker** baking powder	¹/₂	tsp
150 g	all-purpose flour	1¹/₄	cups
4	egg whites	4	

Topping:

1 kg	apricots or cherries, pitted, halved	2	lbs

Decoration:

30 g	icing sugar, sifted	¹/₄	cup

Batter:
PREHEAT oven to 180°C (350°F). Line a
28 x 40 cm (11 x 16") baking sheet with waxed paper.
WHIP butter or margarine until fluffy.
Gradually add sugar, vanilla sugar, egg yolks,
chocolate and rum.
SIFT together baking powder and flour. Stir
into mixture one spoonful at a time.
BEAT egg whites to stiff peaks. Spoon over
butter mixture. Fold into mixture gently but
thoroughly.
SPREAD batter evenly on prepared baking
sheet. (If baking sheet has no rim, fold a piece
of foil in place to prevent expanding dough
from spilling in oven.)

Topping:
COVER batter with apricots or cherries (cut
side face up).
BAKE on middle oven rack for 30-35 minutes.
REMOVE from pan. Let cool completely.

Decoration:
CUT into slices and sprinkle with icing sugar.

Coffee Cake

Recipe No. 538

Batter:

110 g	butter or margarine	¹/₂	cup
200 g	sugar	³/₄	cup
1 pkg	**oetker** vanilla sugar	1	pkg
3	egg yolks	3	
10 mL	**oetker** baking powder	2	tsp
250 g	all-purpose flour	2	cups
125 mL	strong coffee, room temperature	¹/₂	cup
3	egg whites	3	

Soaking:

75 mL	coffee	¹/₃	cup

Filling:

250 mL	whipping cream	1	cup
25 mL	icing sugar	1¹/₂	tbsp
1 pkg	**oetker** Whip it	1	pkg

Apricot Glaze:

125 mL	apricot jam, warm	¹/₂	cup

Coffee Glaze:

250 g	icing sugar, sifted	2¹/₂	cups
45-60 mL	coffee	3-4	tbsp

Batter:
PREHEAT oven to 180°C (350°F). Grease and flour a ring pan.
WHIP butter or margarine until fluffy. Gradually add two-thirds of the sugar, vanilla sugar and egg yolks.
MIX together baking powder and flour. Stir into butter mixture alternately with the coffee.
BEAT egg whites to stiff peaks. Add remaining sugar while beating. Gently fold into batter.
SPREAD batter evenly in prepared pan.
BAKE on lower oven rack for 25-30 minutes.
REMOVE from pan. Let cool completely.
SLICE the cake twice to make three layers.
SOAK each layer, on the cut side, with coffee.
Filling:
COMBINE whipping cream, icing sugar and Whip it. Beat until peaks form.
SPREAD filling over two layers and place together. Top with final layer.
Glaze:
SPREAD warmed apricot jam over cake.
MIX together icing sugar and coffee. Pour over cake.

Plum Sweet Bread

Recipe No. 539

Dough:

500 g	all-purpose flour	3½	cups
1 pkg	**oetker** instant dry yeast	1	pkg
60 g	sugar	¼	cup
1 pkg	**oetker** vanilla sugar	1	pkg
1 mL	salt	¼	tsp
1	egg	1	
2	egg yolks	2	
110 g	butter, melted	½	cup
250 mL	lukewarm milk	1	cup

Filling:

150 mL	plum jam	⅔	cup
30 mL	rum	2	tbsp

Brushing:

50 g	butter, melted	¼	cup

Dough:
GREASE a 25 cm (10") springform pan.
SIFT the flour into a mixing bowl. Add yeast and mix well.
MAKE a well in the centre. Put sugar, vanilla sugar, salt, egg, egg yolks, butter and milk in the well.
KNEAD the dough with an electric mixer fitted with dough hooks until smooth, blistery and no longer sticky.
LET rise, covered, in a warm place, until doubled in size.
KNEAD the dough again. On a floured working surface, shape the dough into a roll, 3 cm (1") in diameter. Cut into 5 cm (2") pieces.
Filling:
MIX together plum jam and rum.
FLATTEN each piece of dough. Place 5 mL (1 tsp) of the jam mixture into the centre of each piece. Press sides together over jam to form a ball.
PLACE each piece into the prepared pan (not too close together).
BRUSH with melted butter. Cover and let rise, until doubled in size.
PREHEAT oven to 180°C (350°F).
BAKE on lower oven rack for 40-45 minutes.

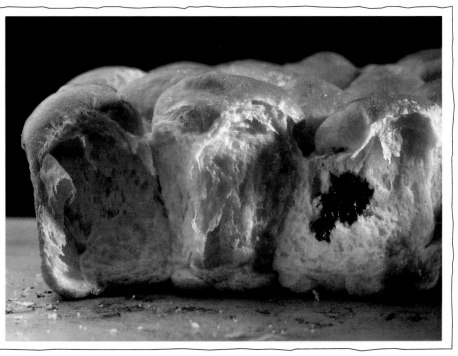

Orange Slices

Recipe No. 540

Dough:

250	g	all-purpose flour	1³/₄ cups
5	mL	**oetker** baking powder	1 tsp
60	g	icing sugar, sifted	¹/₂ cup
1	pkg	**oetker** vanilla sugar	1 pkg
1		egg	1
110	g	cold butter or margarine	¹/₂ cup

Filling:

120	g	almonds, ground	1¹/₃ cups
150	g	sugar	²/₃ cup
		grated peel of 1 orange	
		juice from 1-2 oranges	

Glaze:

100	g	icing sugar, sifted	³/₄ cup
15	mL	orange juice	1 tbsp

Dough:

GREASE a 25 x 30 cm (10 x 12") baking sheet.
MIX together flour and baking powder. Sift onto a working surface.
MAKE a well in the centre. Put icing sugar, vanilla sugar and egg in the well. Add some flour and work into a thick paste.
CUT cold butter or margarine in small pieces over butter mixture. Starting from the centre, work all ingredients into a smooth dough. Let rest for one-half hour.
PREHEAT oven to 160°C (325°F).

Filling:

MIX together ground almonds, sugar and grated orange peel. Stir in enough orange juice so that filling is of spreading consistency.
DIVIDE the dough into two equal parts. Roll out each half to measure 25 x 30 cm (10 x 12").
PLACE one-half of the dough onto the prepared baking sheet. Top evenly with filling. Cover with other half.
BAKE on middle oven rack for 25-30 minutes.

Glaze:

MIX icing sugar with orange juice.
SPREAD on warm pastry. Cut into slices.

Zurich Slices

Recipe No. 541

Batter:

150 g	butter or margarine	²/₃	cup
150 g	sugar	²/₃	cup
1 pkg	**oetker** vanilla sugar	1	pkg
4	egg yolks	4	
5 mL	**oetker** baking powder	1	tsp
100 g	all-purpose flour	³/₄	cup
50 g	almonds, ground	¹/₂	cup
4	egg whites	4	

Filling:

75 mL	apricot jam	¹/₃	cup

Decoration:

30 g	icing sugar	¹/₄	cup

Batter:
PREHEAT oven to 175°C (350°F). Grease a 25 x 30 cm (10 x 12") baking sheet.
WHIP butter or margarine until fluffy. Gradually add sugar, vanilla sugar and egg yolks.
SIFT together baking powder and flour. Stir into the butter mixture one spoonful at a time.
FOLD the almonds into the mixture gently but thoroughly.
BEAT the egg whites to stiff peaks. Spoon over mixture. Fold in gently but thoroughly.
SPREAD the batter evenly onto the prepared pan. (If baking sheet has no rim, fold a piece of foil in place to prevent expanding dough from spilling in oven.)
BAKE on middle oven rack for 25-30 minutes.
REMOVE from pan.
CUT into two equal halves.

Filling:
SPREAD one half with jam. Top with other half.
SPRINKLE with icing sugar and cut into rectangles (3 x 5 cm/1 x 2").

Tea Slices

Recipe No. 542

Batter:

110	g	butter or margarine	¹/₂	cup
140	g	sugar	²/₃	cup
1	pkg	**oetker** vanilla sugar	1	pkg
5		egg yolks	5	
5	mL	**oetker** baking powder	1	tsp
45	g	all-purpose flour	¹/₃	cup
150	g	almonds, ground	1³/₄	cups
5		egg whites	5	

Filling:

75	mL	red currant jam	¹/₃	cup

Glaze:

1	pkg	**oetker** Chocofix	1	pkg

Batter:
PREHEAT oven to 180°C (350°F). Grease a 25 x 30 cm (10 x 12") baking sheet.
WHIP butter or margarine until fluffy. Gradually add sugar, vanilla sugar and egg yolks.
SIFT together baking powder and flour. Stir into butter mixture one spoonful at a time.
GENTLY fold in ground almonds.
BEAT the egg whites to stiff peaks. Spoon over mixture. Fold in gently but thoroughly.
SPREAD batter evenly onto prepared baking sheet. (If baking sheet has no rim, fold a piece of foil in place to prevent expanding dough from spilling in oven.)
BAKE on middle oven rack for 25-30 minutes.
REMOVE from pan. Let cool completely.

Filling:
CUT into two equal halves. Spread one half with jam. Top with other half.

Glaze:
PREPARE Chocofix according to package directions.
GLAZE cake.
BEFORE the glaze sets, use a serrated knife to create a ripple pattern on the surface.
CUT into slices.

Cherry Cake

Recipe No. 543

Batter:

225 g	butter or margarine	1	cup
200 g	sugar	1	cup
1 pkg	**oetker** vanilla sugar	1	pkg
5	egg yolks	5	
3 drops	**oetker** lemon flavouring concentrate	3	drops
5 mL	**oetker** baking powder	1	tsp
200 g	all-purpose flour	1½	cups
5	egg whites	5	

Topping:

	wafers (optional)		
1 kg	cherries, pitted	2	lbs

Decoration:

30 g	icing sugar	¼	cup

Batter:
PREHEAT oven to 180°C (350°F). Grease a 28 x 40 cm (11 x 16") baking sheet.

WHIP the butter or margarine until fluffy. Gradually add sugar, vanilla sugar, egg yolks and flavouring concentrate.
SIFT together baking powder and flour. Stir into butter mixture one spoonful at a time.
BEAT the egg whites to stiff peaks. Spoon over mixture. Fold in gently but thoroughly.
SPREAD the batter evenly (2 cm / ¾" thick) onto the prepared pan. (If baking sheet has no rim, fold a piece of foil in place to prevent expanding dough from spilling in oven.)
Topping:
COVER with cherries.
BAKE on middle oven rack for 25-30 minutes.
REMOVE from pan. Let cool completely.
Decoration:
DECORATE by sprinkling with icing sugar.
CUT into slices.
HINT:
To prevent cherries from sinking into the dough, spread two-thirds of the batter onto the prepared pan. Cover with wafers (these wafers are called Oblaten, and are available from European delicatessens) and spread remaining batter on top. Cover with cherries and bake according to directions.

*P*lum Flan

Recipe No. 544

Batter:

300	g	all-purpose flour	2¼ cups
1	pkg	**oetker** instant dry yeast	1 pkg
1	mL	salt	¼ tsp
15	mL	sugar	1 tbsp
1	pkg	**oetker** vanilla sugar	1 pkg
3	drops	**oetker** lemon flavouring concentrate	3 drops
1		egg	1
30	mL	butter, melted	2 tbsp
125	mL	lukewarm milk	½ cup

Topping:

| 1 | kg | plums, pitted, halved | 2 lbs |

Decoration:

| 15 | mL | cinnamon, sugar, | 1 tbsp |
| | each | icing sugar | each |

Dough:

GREASE a 28 x 40 cm (11 x 16") baking sheet.
SIFT the flour into a mixing bowl. Add yeast and mix well.
MAKE a well in the centre. Put salt, sugar, vanilla sugar, flavouring concentrate, egg, butter and milk in the well.
KNEAD with an electric mixer fitted with dough hooks on high speed until dough is smooth, blistery and no longer sticky.
COVER and let rise, in a warm place, until doubled in size.
ROLL out batter evenly (1 cm / ³/₈") onto prepared pan.

Topping:

COVER completely with halved plums (cut side face up).
SPRINKLE with cinnamon and sugar.
COVER with a towel and let rest for another 20 minutes.
PREHEAT oven to 180°C (350°F).
BAKE on middle oven rack for 45-55 minutes.
REMOVE from pan. Let cool completely.
CUT into slices and sprinkle with icing sugar.

Suggestion:

Instead of plums, apricot halves can be used.

Fruit Slices

Recipe No. 545

Batter:

4	egg yolks	4
80 g	sugar	1/3 cup
1 pkg	**oetker** vanilla sugar	1 pkg
4	egg whites	4
120 g	all-purpose flour	1 cup
pinch	**oetker** baking powder	pinch

Spreading:

45-60 mL	apricot jam	3-4 tbsp

Topping:

	various fruits (bananas, oranges, cherries, etc.)

Glaze:

2 pkgs	**oetker** instant clear glaze	2 pkgs

Decoration:

125 mL	whipping cream	1/2 cup
10 mL	sugar	2 tsp
1/2 pkg	**oetker** Whip it	1/2 pkg

Batter:
PREHEAT oven to 190°C (375°F). Grease a 28 x 40 cm (11 x 16") baking sheet.
WHIP egg yolks until fluffy. Gradually add sugar and vanilla sugar. Continue to whip until mixture is creamy.
BEAT the egg whites to stiff peaks. Spoon over creamed mixture. Fold in gently but thoroughly.
MIX together flour and baking powder. Fold into creamed mixture gently but thoroughly.
SPREAD batter evenly (1 cm / ³/₈" thick) onto prepared pan. (If baking sheet has no rim, fold a piece of foil in place to prevent expanding dough from spilling in oven.)
BAKE on middle oven rack for 10-15 minutes.
LET cake cool in pan.

Spreading and Topping:
SPREAD apricot jam on cooled cake. Cover with fruit.

Glaze:
PREPARE glaze according to package directions. Spoon evenly over fruits. Chill for one-half hour.
CUT into slices.

Decoration:
COMBINE whipping cream, sugar and Whip it. Beat until peaks form.
PUT whipped cream mixture into a pastry bag fitted with a star tube. Decorate fruit slices.

Jelly Roll #1

Recipe No. 546

Batter:

100 g	all-purpose flour	³/₄ cup
5 mL	**oetker** baking powder	1 tsp
1 mL	salt	¹/₄ tsp
3	eggs	3
180 g	sugar	³/₄ cup
50 mL	cold water	¹/₄ cup
1 mL	**oetker** vanilla flavouring concentrate	¹/₄ tsp
some	icing sugar	some

Filling:

125 mL	heated apricot or black currant jam	¹/₂ cup

Decoration:

30 g	icing sugar	¹/₄ cup

Coffee Cream Filling:

125 mL	whipping cream	¹/₂ cup
250 mL	coffee	1 cup
1 pkg	**oetker** vanilla pudding	1 pkg
150 g	sugar	²/₃ cup
225 g	butter, softened	1 cup

Decoration:

12-15	chocolate beans	12-15

Batter:

PREHEAT oven to 190°C (375°F). Grease and line with waxed paper a 25 x 37.5 cm (10 x 15") jelly roll pan.
MIX together flour, baking powder and salt.
BEAT eggs one minute. Gradually add sugar. Continue beating (four minutes) until mixture is thick and light coloured.
ADD water and flavouring concentrate, stirring gently. Fold in dry ingredients.
SPREAD batter in prepared pan.
BAKE on middle oven rack for 12-15 minutes or until top springs back when lightly touched. Immediately loosen edges. Turn out of pan onto a tea towel sprinkled generously with icing sugar.
BRUSH the waxed paper with cold water. Remove carefully but quickly. (For the coffee cream sponge cake: Beginning at the narrow edge, roll cake loosely with towel. Cool on wire rack.)
TRIM crisp edges from cake.

Jam Filling:

SPREAD cake immediately with hot jam.
ROLL up cake quickly and carefully. Cool on wire cake rack. Sprinkle with icing sugar.

Coffee Cream Filling:

ADD whipping cream to coffee.
IN a mixing bowl combine vanilla pudding and sugar.
ADD 125 mL (¹/₂ cup) of the whipping cream-coffee mixture, stirring until smooth.
HEAT the remaining whipping cream-coffee mixture. Remove from heat.
STIR in the pudding mixture. Bring to a boil.
POUR pudding mixture into a bowl and chill. (To prevent skin from forming on the surface, cover with plastic wrap.)
WHIP the butter until light and fluffy.
STIR the butter into the pudding mixture one spoonful at a time.
UNROLL cake carefully and remove towel.
SPREAD one-half of the coffee cream mixture over the cake and roll up.
SPREAD some of the coffee cream on the outside of the roll.
FILL a pastry bag with the remaining coffee cream. Use this and some chocolate beans to decorate the cake.

Jelly Roll #2

Batter:

6	egg whites	6
120 g	icing sugar, sifted	1 cup
1 pkg	**oetker** vanilla sugar	1 pkg
6	egg yolks	6
150 g	all-purpose flour	1 cup
5 mL	**oetker** baking powder	1 tsp
some	icing sugar	some

Chocolate Cream Filling:

1 pkg	**oetker** chocolate pudding	1 pkg
500 mL	milk	2 cups
150 g	sugar	$^2/_3$ cup
15 mL	rum	1 tbsp
225 g	butter	1 cup
	icing sugar	

Vanilla Cream Filling With Fruits:

1 pkg	**oetker** vanilla pudding	1 pkg
500 mL	milk	2 cups
150 g	sugar	$^2/_3$ cup
250-	canned fruit cocktail,	1-
375 mL	thoroughly drained	$1^1/_2$ cups
225 g	butter	1 cup
	icing sugar	

Batter:

PREHEAT oven to 200°C (400°F). Grease and line with waxed paper a 25 x 37.5 cm (10 x 15") jelly roll pan.

BEAT the egg whites to stiff peaks. Gradually add icing sugar and vanilla sugar.

STIR in the egg yolks one at a time.

MIX together flour and baking powder. Sift over the egg yolk mixture. Fold in gently but thoroughly.

SPREAD batter evenly onto the prepared pan.

BAKE on middle oven rack for 12-15 minutes.

REMOVE from pan immediately after baking and turn onto a tea towel sprinkled generously with icing sugar.

BRUSH waxed paper with cold water. Remove it carefully but quickly. Trim crisp edges from cake.

BEGINNING at the narrow edge, roll cake loosely with towel.

COOL on wire rack.

Chocolate Cream Filling:

POUR pudding into a mixing bowl.
ADD 125 mL (¹/₂ cup) of the measured milk and stir until smooth.
IN a saucepan, combine the remaining milk with the sugar. Bring to a boil over medium heat.
REMOVE from heat.
ADD the pudding mixture and return to a boil.
POUR the mixture into a mixing bowl. Fold in rum. (To prevent skin from forming on the surface, cover with plastic wrap.) Chill.
IN another bowl, whip butter until fluffy. Beat in chilled pudding mixture one spoonful at a time.
UNROLL the cooled jelly roll carefully.
Spread with cream. Re-roll, dust with icing sugar.

Vanilla Cream Filling:

POUR pudding into a mixing bowl.
ADD 125 mL (¹/₂ cup) of the measured milk and stir until smooth.
IN a saucepan, combine remaining milk and sugar. Bring to a boil over medium heat.
REMOVE from heat.
ADD the pudding mixture and return to a boil.
POUR the mixture into a mixing bowl. Fold in fruits. (To prevent skin from forming on the surface, cover with plastic wrap.) Chill.
IN another bowl, whip butter until fluffy. Beat in chilled pudding mixture one spoonful at a time.
UNROLL the cooled jelly roll carefully.
Spread with cream. Re-roll, dust with icing sugar.

Hint:

The longer a butter cream is whipped, the fluffier and lighter it becomes.

Battenburg Cake

Recipe No. 547

Batter:

225 g	butter or margarine	1	cup
210 g	sugar	1	cup
1 pkg	**oetker** vanilla sugar	1	pkg
4	eggs	4	
5 mL	**oetker** baking powder	1	tsp
250 g	all-purpose flour	2	cups
15 mL	rum	1	tbsp
45 mL	cocoa	3	tbsp
15 mL	milk	1	tbsp

Spreading:

45-60 mL	apricot jam	3-4	tbsp

Wrapping:

100 g	marzipan	3.5	oz

Batter:

PREHEAT oven to 180°C (350°F). Grease two small straight-sided rectangular cake pans. WHIP butter or margarine until fluffy. Gradually add sugar, vanilla sugar and eggs. SIFT together baking powder and flour. Stir into butter mixture one spoonful at a time. DIVIDE the batter into two portions. TO one portion add rum, cocoa and milk. SPREAD each batter evenly in the prepared pans. BAKE on lower oven rack for 35-40 minutes. REMOVE from pan. Let cool completely. CUT each cake in half lengthwise.

Spreading:

SPREAD evenly with jam. PLACE one dark length next to the white. PLACE the other lengths of cake on top but in reverse. (White on dark, dark on white.)

Wrapping:

ROLL out marzipan evenly. Wrap around cake. Cut into slices.

Almond Cake

Recipe No. 548

Batter:

225	g	butter or margarine	1	cup
200	g	sugar	1	cup
1	pkg	**oetker** vanilla sugar	1	pkg
4		eggs	4	
¹/₂	btl	**oetker** rum flavouring concentrate	¹/₂	btl
pinch		salt		pinch
50	g	**oetker** Gustin corn starch	¹/₃	cup
5	mL	**oetker** baking powder	1	tsp
200	g	all-purpose flour	1¹/₂	cups
100	g	almonds, ground	1	cup
80	g	chocolate chips	¹/₃	cup

Batter:

PREHEAT oven to 160°C (325°F). Grease a loaf pan.

WHIP the butter or margarine until fluffy. Gradually add sugar, vanilla sugar, eggs, flavouring concentrate and salt.

SIFT together corn starch, baking powder and flour. Stir into butter mixture one spoonful at a time.

FOLD in almonds and chocolate chips gently but thoroughly.

SPREAD batter evenly in the prepared pan.

BAKE on lower oven rack for 65-70 minutes. (After the first 15 minutes of baking, make one cut lengthwise along the top surface of the cake.)

REMOVE from pan. Let cool completely.

Hedgehog Cake

Recipe No. 549

Batter:

6	egg whites	6
180 g	sugar	³/₄ cup
1 pkg	**oetker** vanilla sugar	1 pkg
3 drops	**oetker** lemon flavouring concentrate	3 drops
90 g	almonds, finely ground	1 cup
90 g	all-purpose flour	²/₃ cup
70 g	butter, melted	¹/₃ cup

Filling:

75 mL	warm red currant jam	¹/₃ cup

Glaze:

1 pkg	**oetker** Chocofix	1 pkg

Decoration:

55 g	pine nuts	¹/₃ cup

Batter:

PREHEAT oven to 160°C (325°F). Grease a loaf or tube pan and sprinkle with bread crumbs.

BEAT egg whites to stiff peaks. Gradually add sugar, vanilla sugar and flavouring concentrate. Fold into egg white mixture gently but thoroughly.

MIX together almonds and flour. Fold into egg white mixture.

CAREFULLY stir in melted butter.

SPREAD the batter evenly in the prepared pan.

BAKE on lower oven rack for 45-50 minutes.

REMOVE from pan. Let cool completely.

SLICE the cake once to make two layers.

SPREAD jam on bottom layer. Top with second layer.

SPREAD jam over top and sides of cake.

PREPARE Chocofix according to package directions. Glaze cake.

DECORATE with pine nuts.

Quark Slices

Recipe No. 550

Dough:

400	g	all-purpose flour	3 cups
20	mL	**oetker** baking powder	4 tsp
100	g	icing sugar, sifted	³/₄ cup
1	pkg	**oetker** vanilla sugar	1 pkg
1		egg	1
75	mL	milk	¹/₃ cup
110	g	cold butter or margarine	¹/₂ cup

Filling:

4		egg yolks	4
30	mL	hot water	2 tbsp
110	g	sugar	¹/₂ cup
2	pkgs	**oetker** vanilla sugar	2 pkgs
5	drops	**oetker** lemon flavouring concentrate	5 drops
500	g	quark	2 cups
250	mL	whipping cream	1 cup
4		egg whites	4

Brushing:

1		egg yolk	1
5	mL	milk	1 tsp

Dusting:

30	g	icing sugar	¹/₄ cup

Dough:
GREASE a 25 x 36 x 3 cm (10 x 14 x 1") baking sheet.
MIX together flour and baking powder. Sift onto a working surface.
MAKE a well in the centre. Put icing sugar, vanilla sugar, egg and milk in the well. Add some flour and work into a thick paste.
CUT cold butter or margarine into small pieces over the flour mixture.
STARTING from the centre, work all ingredients together to make a smooth dough. Chill for one-half hour.
PREHEAT oven to 180°C (350°F).

Filling:
WHIP egg yolks, water, two-thirds of the sugar, vanilla sugar and flavouring concentrate until fluffy. Gradually add quark and whipping cream.
BEAT the egg whites to stiff peaks. Gradually add the remaining sugar.
FOLD the egg white mixture gently into the quark mixture.
ROLL out one-half of the dough the size of the baking sheet.
ROLL out the remaining dough evenly onto the prepared pan.
SPREAD filling evenly over the dough in the pan. Cover with second layer of dough.

Brushing:
WHISK egg yolk and milk until foamy. Brush on dough surface.
PRICK with fork several times.
BAKE on second lowest oven rack for 30-35 minutes.
COOL. Dust with sieved icing sugar.

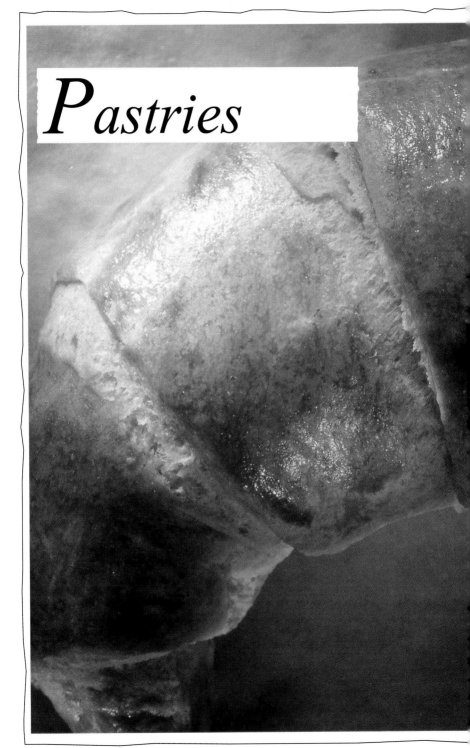

Pastries

Mocha And Nut Boats

Recipe No. 551

Dough:

200 g	all-purpose flour	1½ cups	
5 mL	**oetker** baking powder	1 tsp	
60 g	icing sugar, sifted	½ cup	
1 pkg	**oetker** vanilla sugar	1 pkg	
1	egg	1	
80 g	cold butter or margarine	⅓ cup	

Mocha Cream:

150 g	butter	⅔ cup
100 g	icing sugar, sifted	¾ cup
125 mL	strong coffee	½ cup
30 g	almonds, chopped	¼ cup

Glaze:

220 g	icing sugar, sifted	2 cups
1	egg white	1
15 mL	strong coffee	1 tbsp

Decoration:

mocha beans

Nut Filling:

100 g	walnuts, ground	1 cup
60 g	icing sugar, sifted	½ cup
15 mL	water	1 tbsp

Glaze:

100 g	icing sugar, sifted	¾ cup
3 drops	**oetker** lemon flavouring concentrate	3 drops
15-30 mL	hot water	1-2 tbsp

Decoration:

walnut halves

Dough:

MIX together flour and baking powder. Sift onto a working surface.

MAKE a well in the centre. Put icing sugar, vanilla sugar and egg in the well. Add some flour and work into a thick paste.

CUT the butter or margarine into small pieces over the flour mixture.

STARTING from the centre, work all ingredients into a smooth dough.

CHILL for one hour.

PREHEAT oven to 180°C (350°F).

ROLL out the dough evenly (5 mm / ¼" thick) on the working surface. With a cookie cutter cut out boat shapes. Place on a baking sheet.

BAKE on the middle oven rack for 15-20 minutes.

REMOVE from pan. Let cool completely.

Mocha Cream:

WHIP the butter until very fluffy. Gradually add icing sugar, egg yolk and coffee.

FOLD in almonds gently but thoroughly.

SPREAD the cream over half of the boats. Top with remaining boats.

Glaze:

MIX together icing sugar, egg white and coffee. Stir until smooth.

GLAZE the boats. Decorate with mocha beans.

Nut Filling:

MIX together walnuts and icing sugar. Add only enough water until mixture is easy to spread.

SPREAD filling over half the boats. Top with remaining boats.

Glaze:

PLACE icing sugar in a bowl.

ADD flavouring concentrate. Stir in enough water until mixture is of a thick consistency.

GLAZE the boats. Decorate with walnut halves.

Hazelnut Rounds

Recipe No. 552

Ingredients:

2	egg whites	2
250 g	icing sugar, sifted	2¹/₂ cups
1 pkg	**oetker** vanilla sugar	1 pkg
250 g	hazelnuts, ground	2²/₃ cups

Filling:

80 g	icing sugar	²/₃ cup
30 mL	cocoa	2 tbsp
3 drops	**oetker** almond flavouring concentrate	3 drops
6 drops	**oetker** rum flavouring concentrate	6 drops
2	egg yolks	2
120 g	shortening, room temperature	²/₃ cup

Glaze:

1 pkg	**oetker** Chocofix	1 pkg

Decoration:

hazelnuts or almonds, halved, peeled

Dough:
PREHEAT oven to 120°C (250°F). Lightly grease a baking sheet.
BEAT egg whites to stiff peaks. Gradually add icing sugar and vanilla sugar.
FOLD in half of the nuts gently but thoroughly.
KNEAD enough of the remaining nuts into the mixture until the dough is no longer sticky. (If the mixture is very sticky, add some icing sugar.)
SPRINKLE icing sugar or ground hazelnuts over a working surface.
ROLL out the dough 3 mm (¹/₈") thick.
CUT out round slices (5 cm/2" diameter) with a cookie cutter.
PLACE on prepared baking sheet.
BAKE on middle oven rack for 20-25 minutes.
REMOVE from pan.

Filling:
SIFT icing sugar and cocoa into a mixing bowl.
ADD the flavouring concentrates. Add the egg yolks and shortening.
STIR until mixture is of a smooth consistency. Chill until set.
SPREAD filling on half of the slices. Cover with remaining slices.
SOFTEN Chocofix according to package directions. Glaze slices.
DECORATE with hazelnuts or almonds.

Dessert Fritters

Recipe No. 553

Dough:

300 g	all-purpose flour	2¹/₄	cups
1 pkg	**oetker** instant dry yeast	1	pkg
1 mL	salt	¹/₄	tsp
50 g	sugar	3¹/₂	tbsp
2	egg yolks	2	
50 g	butter, melted	¹/₄	cup
250 mL	lukewarm milk	1	cup

Deep Frying:

	vegetable oil	

Sprinkling:

1 pkg	**oetker** vanilla sugar	1	pkg
30 g	icing sugar, sifted	¹/₄	cup

Sauce:

1 pkg	**oetker** instant vanilla sauce	1	pkg
250 mL	milk	1	cup

Dough:

SIFT the flour into a mixing bowl. Add yeast and mix well.

MAKE a well in the centre. Put salt, sugar, egg yolks, butter and milk in the well.

KNEAD dough with an electric mixer fitted with dough hooks on high speed until dough is smooth, blistery and no longer sticky.

COVER. Let rest, in a warm place, for 30 minutes.

FILL a deep fat fryer half way with oil. Slowly heat the oil (during frying, the temperature of the oil should be a constant 180°C/350°F).

WITH a tablespoon, which is constantly dipped in hot oil, spoon out dough. Deep fry in hot oil until golden. Drain on a paper towel.

Sprinkling:

COMBINE vanilla sugar and icing sugar. Sprinkle over fritters.

Sauce:

PREPARE vanilla sauce according to package directions. Serve along with fritters.

Almond and Raisin Swirls

Recipe No. 554

Dough:

150 g	quark, well drained	²/₃ cup	
75 mL	milk	¹/₃ cup	
1	egg yolk	1	
90 mL	oil	6 tbsp	
80 g	sugar	¹/₃ cup	
1 pkg	**oetker** vanilla sugar	1 pkg	
pinch	salt	pinch	
1 pkg	**oetker** baking powder	1 pkg	
300 g	all-purpose flour	2¹/₄ cups	

Brushing:

1	egg white, beaten	1	

Filling:

50 g	sugar	3¹/₂ tbsp	
1 pkg	**oetker** vanilla sugar	1 pkg	
50 g	currants	¹/₃ cup	
80 g	raisins	²/₃ cup	
50 g	almonds, chopped	¹/₃ cup	

Dough:

PREHEAT oven to 160°C (325°F). Lightly grease a baking sheet.

PLACE the quark in a mixing bowl. Gradually add milk, egg yolk, oil, sugar, vanilla sugar and salt. Stir.

SIFT together baking powder and flour.

STIR two-thirds of the flour mixture into the quark mixture one spoonful at a time.

KNEAD in the remaining flour. (If the dough is sticky add more flour.)

ROLL out the dough into a 45 x 20 cm (18 x 8") rectangle. Brush with beaten egg white.

Filling:

MIX together sugar, vanilla sugar, currants, raisins and almonds. Sprinkle on the dough.

STARTING at the longer side, shape dough into a roll.

CUT into 1.5 cm (⁵/₈") slices. Place on prepared baking sheet.

FLATTEN a little.

BAKE on middle oven rack for 25-30 minutes.

*O*pen Windows

Recipe No. 555

Dough:

500 g	all-purpose flour	3½ cups
5 mL	**oetker** baking powder	1 tsp
100 g	sugar	½ cup
pinch	salt	pinch
½ btl	**oetker** lemon flavouring concentrate	½ btl
3	eggs	3
60 mL	milk	4 tbsp
110 g	cold butter	½ cup

Deep Frying:

	vegetable oil	

Sprinkling:

30 g	icing sugar, sifted	¼ cup

Dough:

SIFT flour and baking powder onto a working surface.

MAKE a well in the centre. Put sugar, salt, flavouring concentrate, eggs and milk in well. Add some flour and work into a thick paste.

CUT the cold butter in small pieces over the flour mixture.

STARTING from the centre, work ingredients into a smooth dough (if dough is sticky add more flour).

ROLL out the dough 2 mm (¹/₁₆") thick. With a cookie cutter, cut out round slices (8 cm / ³/₈" in diameter).

MAKE three lengthwise cuts in each slice (each cut should be 3 cm (1") long and 1 cm (³/₈") apart).

INSERT the handle of a wooden spoon under the cuts and lift through slits.

FILL a deep fat fryer half way with oil. Slowly heat the oil (during frying, the temperature of the oil should be a constant 180°C/350°F).

WITH the wooden spoon, place slices into the hot oil.

FRY the slices until golden brown. Drain on a paper towel.

SPRINKLE with icing sugar.

73

Éclairs

Recipe No. 556

Batter:

250	mL	boiling water	1	cup
110	g	butter or margarine	¹/₂	cup
1	mL	salt	¹/₄	tsp
135	g	all-purpose flour	1	cup
4		eggs	4	

Filling:

250	mL	whipping cream	1	cup
40	g	icing sugar, sifted	¹/₃	cup
1	btl	**oetker** rum flavouring concentrate	1	btl
5	mL	instant coffee	1	tsp
1	pkg	**oetker** Whip it	1	pkg

Glaze:

1	pkg	**oetker** Chocofix	1	pkg

PREHEAT oven to 220°C (425°F).
IN a saucepan bring water, butter or margarine and salt to a boil.
REMOVE from heat and add flour all at once.
STIR constantly over medium heat until mixture forms a ball around the spoon, and pulls away from the sides of the pan. Do not overcook.
PLACE hot dough into a mixing bowl (for faster cooling). Add unbeaten eggs to dough, one at a time, beating thoroughly after each addition. Beat until dough is shiny and no longer sticky.
PUT mixture into a pastry bag fitted with a star tube. Squeeze 2.5 x 7.5 cm (1 x 3") strips onto an ungreased baking sheet.
BAKE on middle oven rack for 30-35 minutes. (Do not open oven door during first fifteen minutes of baking, dough may collapse.)
WHILE éclairs are still warm, cut in half lengthwise. Let cool.

Filling:
WHIP the cream with remaining filling ingredients until peaks form.
PIPE filling into bottom halves of éclairs.

Glaze:
SOFTEN the Chocofix according to package directions.
Glaze top half of each éclair.
COVER bottoms with glazed top halves.

74

Choux Pastries

Recipe No. 557

Dough: Basic Recipe

250 mL	water	1 cup
110 g	butter	¹/₂ cup
1 mL	salt	¹/₄ tsp
135 g	all-purpose flour	1 cup
4	eggs	4

Dough:

PREHEAT oven to 220°C (425°F).
IN a saucepan bring water, butter and salt to a boil.
REMOVE from heat and add flour all at once.
STIR over medium heat until mixture forms a ball around the spoon, and pulls away from the sides of the pan. (Do not overcook.)
COOL slightly.
ADD unbeaten eggs to dough one at a time, stirring after each addition until smooth. Beat until mixture is shiny and no longer sticky.
CHILL until mixture holds its shape.
PUT mixture into a pastry bag fitted with a star tube. Squeeze portions the size of a small mandarin orange onto an ungreased baking sheet.
BAKE on middle oven rack for 25-30 minutes. (Do not open oven door during first fifteen minutes of baking, pastry may collapse.)
WHILE pastries are still warm, cut in half. Let cool and fill.

Vanilla Pastries

Filling:

2 pkgs	**oetker** vanilla pudding	2 pkgs
80 g	sugar	¹/₃ cup
1 L	milk	4 cups

Sprinkle:

| 30 g | icing sugar | ¹/₄ cup |

Filling:

PREPARE pudding according to package directions.
POUR into a bowl. Cover with plastic wrap and chill.
SHORTLY before serving, pipe filling into bottom halves of pastries and cover with top halves.
SPRINKLE with icing sugar.

Strawberry Pastries

Filling:

875 mL	strawberries	3¹/₂ cups
1 pkg	**oetker** vanilla sugar	1 pkg
15 mL	lemon juice	1 tbsp
250 mL	whipping cream	1 cup
70 g	sugar	¹/₄ cup
1 pkg	**oetker** Whip it	1 pkg

Sprinkling:

| 30 g | icing sugar | ¹/₄ cup |

Filling:

WASH the strawberries. Cut into small pieces.
SPRINKLE with vanilla sugar and lemon juice.
COVER and let rest for a short time.
COMBINE whipping cream, sugar and Whip it. Beat until peaks form.
PUT into pastry bag.
SHORTLY before serving, fill each bottom half with 15 mL (1 tbsp) of strawberries.
PIPE whipping cream over top of the strawberries.
COVER with top halves of pastry. Sprinkle with icing sugar.

Chocolate Pastries

Filling:

1 pkg	**oetker** chocolate pudding	1 pkg	
30-60 mL	sugar	2-4 tbsp	
500 mL	milk	2 cups	
50 g	semi-sweet chocolate, grated	2 squares	
1 pkg	**oetker** Whip it	1 pkg	
125 mL	whipping cream	½ cup	

Glaze:

1 pkg	**oetker** Chocofix	1 pkg	

Filling:
PREPARE pudding according to package directions.
POUR into a bowl. Cover with plastic wrap and chill.
STIR grated chocolate into the chilled pudding.
ADD Whip it to the whipping cream. Beat until peaks form.
STIR into pudding mixture.
PUT into pastry bag.
FILL bottom halves of pastry with the chocolate cream.

Glaze:
PREPARE Chocofix according to package directions. Glaze the top halves.
PLACE on filled bottom halves.

Filled Choux Pastry Rings

Recipe No. 558

Dough:
125 mL	boiling water	$^1/_2$ cup
60 g	butter	$^1/_4$ cup
pinch	salt	pinch
65 g	all-purpose flour	$^1/_2$ cup
2	eggs	2

Filling:
500 mL	blueberries or raspberries	2 cups
1 pkg	**oetker** vanilla sugar	1 pkg
250 mL	whipping cream	1 cup
70 g	sugar	$^1/_4$ cup
1 pkg	**oetker** Whip it	1 pkg

Glaze:
250 g	icing sugar	$2^1/_2$ cups
45-60 mL	rum	3-4 tbsp

Dough:
PREHEAT oven to 200°C (425°F).
IN a saucepan, bring water, butter and salt to a boil.
REMOVE from heat and add flour all at once.
STIR constantly over medium heat until mixture forms a ball around the spoon, and pulls away from the sides of the pan (approximately 1 minute); do not overcook.
PLACE hot dough into a mixing bowl and cool slightly. Add unbeaten eggs to dough one at a time, stirring thoroughly after each addition.
Beat mixture until shiny and no longer sticky.
Chill until mixture holds its shape.
PUT dough into a pastry bag fitted with a star tube. Squeeze 8 cm (3") filled circles onto an ungreased baking sheet. Squeeze a ring on top of the circle.
BAKE on middle oven rack for 20-25 minutes. (Do not open oven door during the first fifteen minutes of baking, pastry may collapse.)
WHILE pastry is still warm, slice off the top of the ring.

Filling:
WASH blueberries or raspberries thoroughly and sprinkle with vanilla sugar.
COMBINE whipping cream, sugar and Whip it. Beat until peaks form.
FOLD in fruit gently but thoroughly.

Glaze:
SIFT icing sugar into a bowl. Gradually add rum, stirring until mixture is of spreading consistency.
GLAZE the top ring.
SHORTLY before serving, fill the circles with the fruit mixture and top with glazed rings.

*N*ut Filled Crescents

Recipe No. 559

Dough:

150 g	quark, well drained	²/₃	cup
45 mL	milk	3	tbsp
1	egg	1	
90 mL	oil	6	tbsp
80 g	sugar	¹/₃	cup
1 pkg	**oetker** vanilla sugar	1	pkg
pinch	salt		pinch
300 g	all-purpose flour	2¹/₄	cups
1 pkg	**oetker** baking powder	1	pkg

Filling:

100 g	hazelnuts, ground	1	cup
70 g	sugar	¹/₄	cup
2 drops	**oetker** almond flavouring concentrate	2	drops
1	egg white	1	
some	water		some

Brushing:

1	egg yolk	1	
5 mL	milk	1	tsp

Dough:
PREHEAT oven to 180°C (350°F).
PUT the well-drained quark into a mixing bowl. Gradually add milk, egg, oil, sugar, vanilla sugar and salt. Mix well.
SIFT together flour and baking powder.
FOLD into quark mixture, gently but thoroughly, one spoonful at a time. (Should dough be sticky, add some more flour.)

Filling:
COMBINE hazelnuts, sugar, flavouring concentrate and egg white.
STIR in just enough water until mixture becomes creamy.
ROLL out dough thinly and cut into circles the size of a 26 cm (10") springform pan bottom.
Cut each circle into halves, then quarters and finally eighths.
STARTING at the broader end, place a small amount of filling on the dough and roll up. Shape into crescents.
PLACE crescents on a baking sheet.
WHISK egg yolk and milk until foamy. Brush crescents with milk mixture.
BAKE on middle oven rack for 20-25 minutes.

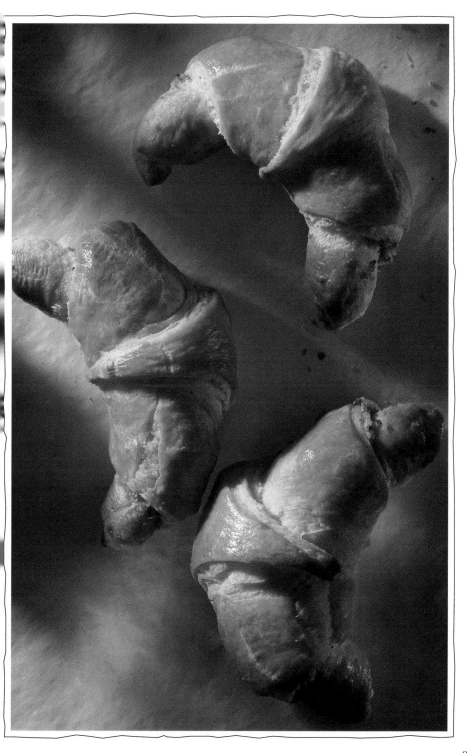

Savoury Choux Pastries

Recipe No. 560

Dough:

125 mL	boiling water	1/2 cup	
60 g	butter or margarine	1/4 cup	
pinch	salt	pinch	
65 g	all-purpose flour	1/2 cup	
2	eggs	2	

Cheese Filling:

80 g	cream cheese, softened	1/3 cup	
2 wedges	processed cheese (foil triangles), shredded	2 wedges	
pinch	salt, pepper, paprika	pinch	

Ham Filling:

100 g	cooked ham	4 oz	
1	egg, hard-boiled	1	
2	gherkins	2	
pinch	salt	pinch	
15 mL	sour cream	1 tbsp	

Quark Filling:

200 g	quark	3/4 cup	
15-30 mL	sour cream	1-2 tbsp	
pinch	salt, pepper	pinch	
15 mL	chives, chopped	1 tbsp	
15 mL	parsley, chopped	1 tbsp	

Decoration:

some	cherry tomatoes	some	
4-5	radishes, apple slices, watercress, parsley, grapes, etc.	4-5	

Dough:

PREHEAT oven to 220°C (425°F).
IN a saucepan, bring water, butter or margarine and salt to a boil.
REMOVE from heat and add flour all at once.
STIR constantly over medium heat until mixture forms a ball around the spoon and pulls away from the sides of the pan (approximately 1 minute); do not overcook.
PLACE hot dough into a mixing bowl and coo. slightly. Add unbeaten eggs to the dough one at a time, stirring thoroughly after each addition. Beat mixture until shiny and no longer sticky. Chill until mixture holds its shape.
PUT dough into a pastry bag fitted with a star tube. Squeeze twenty-four small balls, the size of a walnut, onto an ungreased baking sheet.
BAKE on middle oven rack until puffs have doubled in size and are beginning to brown (5-10 minutes for small, 15 minutes for medium, 20 minutes for large). (Do not open oven door during the first fifteen minutes of baking, pastry may collapse.)
REDUCE temperature to 180°C (350°F). Bake until crisp and light brown.
TURN off heat. Cut a slit in each puff and return to oven for 10 minutes. Remove puffs from oven when tops are crisp and only a few threads of moisture are found inside.
WHILE the pastry is still warm, cut in half.

Cheese Filling:

MIX together the two cheeses. Stir until smooth.
SEASON with salt, pepper and paprika.

Ham Filling:

CUT ham, egg and gherkins into small cubes. Add salt.
ADD sour cream and mix well.

Quark Filling:

STRAIN the quark. Add sour cream and beat until smooth.
ADD salt, pepper, chives and parsley and stir well.
FILL one-third of pastries with a different filling and cover.
DECORATE.

Cheese Filled Pastries

Recipe No. 561

Dough:

200 g	all-purpose flour	1½ cups
50 g	**oetker** Gustin corn starch	⅓ cup
5 mL	**oetker** baking powder	1 tsp
pinch	salt	pinch
1	egg white	1
½	egg yolk	½
30 mL	water	2 tbsp
110 g	cold butter or margarine	½ cup

Brushing:

| ½ | egg yolk | ½ |
| 5 mL | milk | 1 tsp |

Decoration:

| some | parmesan cheese, grated, caraway or poppy seeds, walnuts, parsley | some |

Filling:

50 g	butter	¼ cup
2 wedges	processed cheese (foil triangles), shredded	2 wedges
pinch	salt, paprika	pinch

Dough:
MIX together flour, corn starch and baking powder.
SIFT onto a working surface.
MAKE a well in the centre. Put salt, egg white, one-half egg yolk and water in the well.
ADD some flour and work into a thick paste.
CUT the butter or margarine in small pieces over the flour mixture.
STARTING at the centre, work all ingredients together into a smooth dough.
CHILL for one-half hour.
PREHEAT oven to 175°C (350°F).
ROLL out dough to a 3 mm (⅛") thickness.
CUT into 4 x 4 cm (1½ x 1½") squares. Place on a baking sheet.
COMBINE one-half egg yolk and milk.
WHISK together.
BRUSH each square with the milk mixture.
DECORATE one-half of the squares with parmesan cheese, caraway seeds or poppy seeds. These will become the tops.
BAKE on middle oven rack for 10-15 minutes.

Filling:
WHIP butter until fluffy. Gradually add the shredded cheese.
SEASON with salt and paprika. Stir well.
SPREAD cheese filling on the underside of one-half of the cooled squares.
COVER with tops.

85

*H*am Crescents

Recipe No. 562

Dough:

250 g	all-purpose flour	1¼	cups
10 mL	**oetker** baking powder	2	tsp
pinch	salt		pinch
1	egg	1	
225 g	cold butter or margarine	1	cup
250 g	quark	1	cup

Filling:

150 g	ham	6	oz
2	eggs, hard-boiled	2	
3	small gherkins	3	
45 mL	pimento	3	tbsp
15 mL	Dijon mustard	1	tbsp
pinch	salt, pepper		pinch
15 mL	parsley, chopped	1	tbsp
15 mL	sour cream	1	tbsp

Brushing:

30 mL	milk	2	tbsp

Dough:

RINSE a baking sheet with cold water.
MIX together flour and baking powder.
SIFT onto a working surface.
MAKE a well in the centre. Put salt and egg in the well.
ADD some flour and work into a thick paste.
CUT the butter or margarine in small pieces over the flour mixture.
SPOON the quark over top.
STARTING from the centre, work all ingredients into a smooth dough.
CHILL for one-half hour.
KNEAD well again.
CHILL again for one-half hour.
PREHEAT oven to 180°C (350°F).
ROLL out dough to a 2 mm (¹/₁₆") thickness.
USING a pizza cutter, cut out circles the size of a 26 cm (10") springform pan.
SLICE each circle four times (first into halves, then into quarters, finally into eighths).

Filling:

CHOP ham, eggs, gherkins and pimento into fine pieces.
ADD mustard, salt, pepper, parsley and sour cream.
STIR well.
BRUSH the tips of each one-eighth piece of dough with milk.
STARTING at the broader end, place some filling on the piece of dough and roll up to form a crescent. Repeat until all pieces have been filled.
BRUSH each crescent with milk and place on prepared baking sheet.
BAKE on middle oven rack for 20-25 minutes.

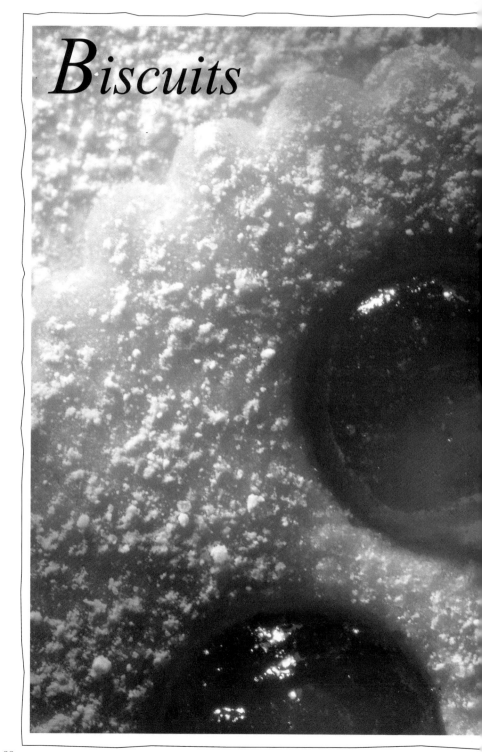

Biscuits

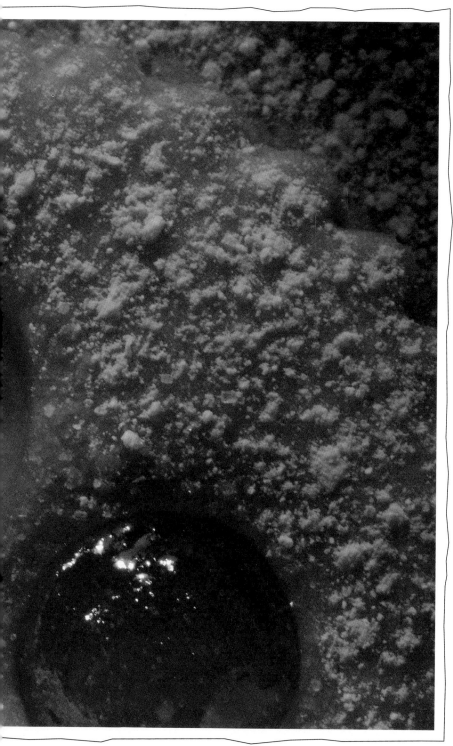

Linzer Cookies

Recipe No. 563

Dough:

600 g	all-purpose flour	4¹/₂	cups
220 g	icing sugar, sifted	2	cups
2 pkgs	**oetker** vanilla sugar	2	pkgs
4	egg yolks	4	
400 g	cold butter or margarine	1³/₄	cups

Spreading:

125 mL	apricot jam, strained	¹/₂	cup

Sprinkling:

30 g	icing sugar	¹/₄	cup

Dough:
SIFT flour onto a working surface.
MAKE a well in the centre. Put icing sugar, vanilla sugar and egg yolks in the well.
ADD some flour and work into a thick paste.
CUT butter or margarine in small pieces over the flour mixture.
STARTING at the centre, work all ingredients into a smooth dough.
CHILL for one-half hour.
PREHEAT oven to 180°C (350°F).
ROLL out dough thinly.
WITH a round cookie cutter, cut out slices, 5 cm (2") in diameter.
ON one-half of the slices, cut out three holes in each slice.
PLACE all slices on a baking sheet.
BAKE on middle oven rack for 10-12 minutes.
REMOVE from baking sheet.
SPREAD the underside of all the slices without holes with jam.
SPRINKLE icing sugar over the slices with holes and sandwich together.

Vanilla Crescents

Recipe No. 564

Dough:

300 g	all-purpose flour	2¹/₄	cups
110 g	hazelnuts, ground	1¹/₄	cups
60 g	icing sugar, sifted	¹/₂	cup
1 pkg	**oetker** vanilla sugar	1	pkg
225 g	cold butter or margarine	1	cup

For Rolling:

150 g	icing sugar, sifted	1¹/₃	cups
1-2 pkgs	**oetker** vanilla sugar	1-2	pkgs

Dough:
PREHEAT oven to 160°C (325°F).
SIFT the flour onto a working surface.
MIX in ground nuts, icing sugar and vanilla sugar.
CUT the butter or margarine in small pieces over the nut mixture.
STARTING at the centre, work all ingredients into a smooth dough.
IF the dough is too crumbly, add 5-10 mL (1-2 tsp) of milk.
SHAPE the dough into rolls the size of a pencil.
CUT into 5 cm (2") long pieces. Shape into crescents. Place on a baking sheet.
BAKE on middle oven rack for 20 minutes.
REMOVE from baking sheet.
MIX together icing sugar and vanilla sugar.
ROLL crescents in sugar mixture while still hot.

*F*riends Of The Family

Recipe No. 565

Batter:

3	eggs	3	
140 g	sugar	²/₃	cup
1 pkg	**oetker** vanilla sugar	1	pkg
100 g	all-purpose flour	³/₄	cup
1 mL	**oetker** baking powder	¹/₄	tsp
100 g	hazelnuts, coarsely chopped	³/₄	cup
100 g	raisins	³/₄	cup
50 g	candied lemon peel, chopped	¹/₄	cup
50 g	candied orange peel, chopped	¹/₄	cup
30 g	glacé cherries, chopped	¹/₄	cup

Batter:
PREHEAT oven to 160°C (325°F). Lightly grease and flour a 25 x 30 cm (10 x 12") baking sheet.
WHIP eggs until fluffy.
GRADUALLY add sugar and vanilla sugar.
CONTINUE to beat until mixture is creamy.
MIX together flour and baking powder.
SIFT over creamed mixture.
PLACE fruit on top.
FOLD in flour and fruit gently but thoroughly.
SPREAD batter 1 cm (³/₈") thick on the prepared baking sheet. (If baking sheet has no rim, fold a piece of foil in place to prevent expanding batter from spilling in oven.)
BAKE on middle oven rack for 20-25 minutes.
REMOVE from baking sheet.
CUT into small slices while still hot.

Meringues

ecipe No. 566

ngredients:

3	egg whites	3
70 g	sugar	¹/₄ cup
1 mL	cream of tartar	¹/₈ tsp
120 g	icing sugar	1 cup

Sprinkling:

sugar sprinkles,
chocolate sprinkles,
cherries

Decoration:

some   chocolate, softened   some

Meringue Mixture:

PREHEAT oven to 70°C (150°F).

BEAT egg whites to stiff peaks. (Peaks should be so stiff that when a knife is inserted, the cut remains visible.)

GRADUALLY add sugar and cream of tartar. Continue beating until mixture is white and shiny.

SIFT icing sugar over egg white mixture. Fold in gently but thoroughly.

PUT mixture into a pastry bag fitted with a star tube.

SQUEEZE desired shapes on a baking sheet.

SPRINKLE with sugar and chocolate sprinkles.

BAKE on middle oven rack for one and one-half hour.

REMOVE from baking sheet.

DECORATE as desired.

(To store, make sure meringues have completely cooled after baking. Keep in a container with a tight-fitting lid.)

Delicate "S"

Recipe No. 567

Dough:

250 g	all-purpose flour	1³/₄	cups
15 mL	**oetker** baking powder	1	tbsp
80 g	icing sugar, sifted	²/₃	cup
1 pkg	**oetker** vanilla sugar	1	pkg
1	egg	1	
1	egg yolk	1	
110 g	cold butter or margarine	¹/₂	cup

Decoration:

1	egg white	1	
50 g	almonds, thinly sliced	¹/₃	cup

Dough:

MIX together flour and baking powder.
SIFT onto a working surface.
MAKE a well in the centre. Put icing sugar, vanilla sugar, egg and egg yolk in the well.
WORK into a thick paste.
CUT the butter or margarine in small pieces over the sugar mixture.
STARTING from the centre, work all ingredients into a smooth dough.
CHILL for one-half hour.
PREHEAT oven to 180°C (350°F).
SHAPE dough into rolls (the thickness of a pencil).
CUT into 10 cm (4") long pieces.
BEAT egg white with a fork.
DIP each piece of dough in the egg white mixture. Roll in sliced almonds until covered.
SHAPE each roll into an "S" and place on a baking sheet.
BAKE on middle oven rack for 15-20 minutes.

Rolled Oat Kisses

Recipe No. 568

Ingredients:

140 g	rolled oats	1½	cups
50 g	hazelnuts, chopped	⅓	cup
30 mL	oil	2	tbsp
2	egg whites	2	
140 g	sugar	⅔	cup

Oat Mixture:
PREHEAT oven to 150°C (300°F). Lightly grease a baking sheet.
IN a skillet, over medium heat, toast rolled oats and nuts in oil until golden brown.
LET cool completely.
BEAT the egg whites to stiff peaks.
GRADUALLY add sugar.
CAREFULLY fold in toasted oats and nuts.
USING a teaspoon, scoop out spoonfuls of the mixture and place on prepared baking sheet.
BAKE on middle oven rack for 20-25 minutes.

conut Kisses

Nutty Kisses

Recipe No. 570

Ingredients:

4	egg whites	4
200 g	sugar	1 cup
1 pkg	**oetker** vanilla sugar	1 pkg
1 mL	cinnamon	¹/₄ tsp
2 drops	**oetker** almond flavouring concentrate	2 drops
200 g	coconut, shredded	2 cups

Coconut Mixture:
PREHEAT oven to 120°C (250°F). Lightly grease a baking sheet.
BEAT egg whites to very stiff peaks. (Peaks should be so stiff that when a knife is inserted, the cut remains visible.)
GRADUALLY fold in sugar and vanilla sugar.
ADD cinnamon and flavouring concentrate.
FOLD shredded coconut into egg white mixture gently but thoroughly.
USING two teaspoons, scoop out portions of the mixture. Place on the prepared baking sheet.
BAKE on middle oven rack for 30-40 minutes.

Ingredients:

125 g	walnuts, ground	1¹/₃ cups
250 g	sugar	1 cup
3	egg whites	3
1 mL	cinnamon	¹/₄ tsp
3 drops	**oetker** lemon flavouring concentrate	3 drops
	round baking wafers	

Decoration:
walnuts or hazelnuts

Nut Mixture:
PREHEAT oven to 160°C (325°F). Lightly grease a baking sheet.
USING a double boiler, combine ground nuts, sugar, egg whites, cinnamon and flavouring concentrate.
STIRRING constantly, heat to 40°C (104°F).
REMOVE from heat and let cool completely.
PUT nut mixture into a pastry bag and squeeze little portions on each of the baking wafers.
PLACE a hazelnut in the centre of each portion.
PLACE on prepared baking sheet.
BAKE on lowest oven rack for 20-25 minutes.

Lemon Spritz Cookies

Recipe No. 571

Dough:

225	g	butter or margarine	1 cup
120	g	icing sugar, sifted	1 cup
1	pkg	**oetker** vanilla sugar	1 pkg
2		eggs	2
¹/₂	btl	**oetker** lemon flavouring concentrate	¹/₂ btl
350	g	all-purpose flour	2¹/₂ cups
15	mL	**oetker** baking powder	1 tbsp

Decoration:

nuts, raisins, candied fruit, **oetker** Chocofix

Dough:

PREHEAT oven to 160°C (325°F).
WHIP butter or margarine until fluffy.
GRADUALLY add icing sugar, vanilla sugar, eggs and flavouring concentrate.
SIFT together flour and baking powder.
FOLD into butter mixture one spoonful at a time.
PUT mixture into a pastry bag fitted with a star tube.
SQUEEZE desired shapes onto a baking sheet.
DECORATE as desired.
BAKE on middle oven rack for 10-15 minutes.

Chocolate Spritz Cookies

Recipe No. 572

Dough:

225	g	butter or margarine	1 cup
120	g	icing sugar, sifted	1 cup
1	pkg	**oetker** vanilla sugar	1 pkg
1		egg white	1
300	g	all-purpose flour	2¼ cups
10	mL	**oetker** baking powder	2 tsp
50	g	almonds, ground	½ cup
50	g	semi-sweet chocolate, grated	2 squares

Decoration:

nuts, raisins, candied fruit

Dough:
PREHEAT oven to 160°C (325°F).
WHIP the butter or margarine until fluffy.
GRADUALLY add icing sugar, vanilla sugar and egg white.
SIFT together flour and baking powder.
FOLD into butter mixture one spoonful at a time.
FOLD almonds and chocolate into mixture gently but thoroughly.
PUT mixture into a pastry bag fitted with a star tube.
SQUEEZE desired shapes onto a baking sheet.
DECORATE as desired.
BAKE on middle oven rack for 10-15 minutes.

Macaroons

Recipe No. 573

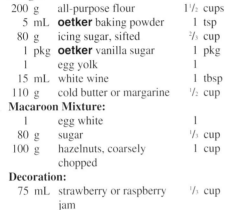

Dough:

200 g	all-purpose flour	1½	cups
5 mL	**oetker** baking powder	1	tsp
80 g	icing sugar, sifted	⅔	cup
1 pkg	**oetker** vanilla sugar	1	pkg
1	egg yolk	1	
15 mL	white wine	1	tbsp
110 g	cold butter or margarine	½	cup

Macaroon Mixture:

1	egg white	1	
80 g	sugar	⅓	cup
100 g	hazelnuts, coarsely chopped	1	cup

Decoration:

75 mL	strawberry or raspberry jam	⅓	cup

Dough:

MIX together flour and baking powder.
SIFT onto a working surface.
MAKE a well in the centre. Put icing sugar, vanilla sugar, egg yolk and wine in the well.
ADD some flour and work into a thick paste.
CUT the butter or margarine in small pieces over the flour mixture.
STARTING at the centre, work all ingredients into a smooth dough.
CHILL for one-half hour.
PREHEAT oven to 165°C (325°F).
ROLL out dough thinly.
USING a round cookie cutter, cut out slices 5 cm (2") in diameter.
PLACE cookies on a baking sheet.

Macaroon Mixture:

WHIP the egg white to stiff peaks.
FOLD sugar and nuts gently into egg white mixture.
USING a teaspoon, scoop out portions of the mixture and place on each cookie.
MAKE a small well in the centre of the macaroon and fill with jam.
BAKE on middle oven rack for 15-20 minutes.

Chocolate Nut Cookies

Recipe No. 574

Dough:

160 g	all-purpose flour	1¼ cups	
5 mL	**oetker** baking powder	1 tsp	
140 g	sugar	⅔ cup	
1 pkg	**oetker** vanilla sugar	1 pkg	
1	egg	1	
110 g	cold butter or margarine	½ cup	
100 g	semi-sweet chocolate, grated	4 squares	
100 g	almonds, ground	1 cup	

Lemon Glaze:

80 g	icing sugar	⅔ cup
10 mL	lemon juice	2 tsp

Decoration:

30-35	chocolates	30-35

Dough:

MIX together flour and baking powder.
SIFT onto a working surface.
MAKE a well in the centre. Put sugar, vanilla sugar and egg in the well.
ADD some flour and work into a thick paste.
CUT the butter or margarine into small pieces over the flour mixture.
ADD the chocolate and almonds.
STARTING from the centre, work all ingredients into a smooth dough.
CHILL for one-half hour.
PREHEAT oven to 160°C (325°F).
ROLL out dough thinly.
USING a round cookie cutter, cut out slices 3-4 cm (1-1½") in diameter.
PLACE slices on a baking sheet.
BAKE on middle oven rack for 10-15 minutes.
REMOVE from pan. Let cool completely.

Glaze:

SIFT icing sugar into a bowl.
ADD lemon juice.
ADD enough water and stir until mixture is thick.
BRUSH some lemon glaze on each slice.
PLACE a chocolate in each centre.
LET dry.

*A*lmond Pillows

Recipe No. 575

Dough:

200 g	all-purpose flour	1¹/₂ cups	
pinch	salt	pinch	
60 g	almonds, ground	²/₃ cup	
50 g	semi-sweet chocolate, grated	2 squares	
100 g	sugar	¹/₂ cup	
1 pkg	**oetker** vanilla sugar	1 pkg	
1	egg	1	
60 g	cold butter	¹/₂ cup	

Glaze:

30 mL	water	2 tbsp	
2 drops	**oetker** lemon flavouring concentrate	2 drops	
1-2 drops	yellow food colour	1-2 drops	
160 g	icing sugar, sifted	1¹/₃ cups	

Dough:

SIFT flour onto a working surface.
SPRINKLE salt, almonds and grated chocolate over the flour.
MAKE a well in the centre. Put sugar, vanilla sugar and egg in the well.
ADD some flour and work into a thick paste.
CUT the butter in small pieces over the flour mixture.
STARTING from the centre, work all ingredients into a smooth dough.
CHILL for one-half hour.
PREHEAT oven to 160°C (325°F).
ROLL out dough thinly.
CUT out shapes.
PLACE on a baking sheet.
BAKE on middle oven rack for 10-15 minutes.
LET cool completely.

Glaze:

ADD water, flavouring concentrate and food colour to the icing sugar. Stir until smooth.

*A*lmond Delights

Recipe No. 576

Dough:

200 g	all-purpose flour	1¹/₂ cups	
2 mL	**oetker** baking powder	¹/₂ tsp	
70 g	sugar	¹/₄ cup	
1 pkg	**oetker** vanilla sugar	1 pkg	
1	egg	1	
3 drops	**oetker** almond flavouring concentrate	3 drops	
110 g	cold butter or margarine	¹/₂ cup	

Topping:

1	egg	1	
100 g	almonds, sliced	²/₃ cup	
70 g	sugar	¹/₄ cup	

Dough:

MIX together flour and baking powder.
SIFT onto a working surface.
MAKE a well in the centre. Put sugar, vanilla sugar, egg and flavouring concentrate in the well.
ADD some flour and work into a thick paste.
CUT butter or margarine in small pieces over the flour mixture.
STARTING from the centre, work all ingredients into a smooth dough.
CHILL for one-half hour.
PREHEAT oven to 180°C (350°F).
ROLL out dough to a ¹/₂ cm (¹/₄") thickness.
USING a round cookie cutter, cut out cookies 3 cm (1") in diameter.
PLACE cookies on a baking sheet.
WHISK the egg.
BRUSH each cookie with the egg mixture.

Topping:

MIX together almonds and sugar.
SPRINKLE almond mixture on each cookie.
BAKE on middle oven rack for 10-12 minutes.

Glazed Wine Cookies

Recipe No. 577

Dough:

200	g	all-purpose flour	1¹/₂	cups
10	mL	**oetker** baking powder	2	tsp
100	g	sugar	¹/₂	cup
1	pkg	**oetker** vanilla sugar	1	pkg
1		egg	1	
45	mL	white wine	3	tbsp
110	g	cold butter or margarine	¹/₂	cup
25	g	semi-sweet chocolate, grated	1	square

Glaze:

150	g	icing sugar	1¹/₃	cups
15-30	mL	white wine	1-2	tbsp

Decoration:

100	g	candied fruit	²/₃	cup

Dough:

MIX together flour and baking powder.
SIFT onto a working surface.
MAKE a well in the centre. Put sugar, vanilla sugar, egg and wine in the well.
ADD some flour and work into a thick paste.
CUT the cold butter or margarine in small pieces over the flour mixture.
ADD the grated chocolate.
STARTING from the centre, work all ingredients into a smooth dough.
CHILL for one-half hour.
PREHEAT oven to 180°C (350°F).
ROLL out dough thinly.
USING a round cookie cutter, cut out slices 3-4 cm (1-1¹/₂") in diameter.
PLACE cookies on a baking sheet.
BAKE on middle oven rack for 10-15 minutes.
LET cool completely.

Glaze:

SIFT the icing sugar into a mixing bowl.
ADD enough wine and stir until mixture is thick.
COVER the cookies with the glaze.
DECORATE with the candied fruit.

Chocolate Glazed Beret

Recipe No. 578

Dough:

200 g	all-purpose flour	1½ cups	
5 mL	**oetker** baking powder	1 tsp	
180 g	cold butter	¾ cup	
100 g	icing sugar, sifted	¾ cup	
1 pkg	**oetker** vanilla sugar	1 pkg	
100 g	almonds, ground	1 cup	

Filling:

60 mL	apricot jam	¼ cup	

Glaze:

1 pkg	**oetker** Chocofix	1 pkg	

Decoration:

40 g	pistachio nuts	¼ cup	

Dough:

MIX together flour and baking powder.
SIFT onto a working surface.
CUT the butter in small pieces.
MAKE a well in the centre. Put icing sugar, vanilla sugar, butter and almonds in the well.
COVER with flour.
STARTING from the centre, work all ingredients into a smooth dough.
CHILL for one-half hour.
PREHEAT oven to 200°C (400°F).
ROLL out dough to ½ cm (³/₁₆") thickness.
USING a round cutter, cut out cookies 5 cm (2") in diameter.
PLACE cookies on a baking sheet.
BAKE on middle oven rack for 10-15 minutes.
LET cool completely.
SPREAD the underside of each cookie with jam. Sandwich together.
PREPARE Chocofix according to package directions.
GLAZE each cookie. Decorate with pistachio nuts.

Almond Bars

Recipe No. 579

Dough:

200	g	all-purpose flour	1½	cups
½	pkg	**oetker** baking powder	½	pkg
100	g	sugar	½	cup
2		egg yolks	2	
60	mL	milk	¼	cup
110	g	cold butter or margarine	½	cup
100	g	almonds, sliced	¾	cup

Filling:

75	mL	red currant jam	⅓	cup

Decoration:

½	pkg	**oetker** Chocofix	½	pkg

Dough:

MIX together flour and baking powder.
SIFT onto a working surface.
MAKE a well in the centre. Put sugar, egg yolks and milk in the well.
ADD some flour and work into a thick paste.
CUT cold butter or margarine in small pieces over the flour mixture.
STARTING from the centre, work all ingredients into a smooth dough.
KNEAD almonds into the mixture.
CHILL for one-half hour.
PREHEAT oven to 180°C (350°F).
ROLL out dough to a 3 mm (⅛") thickness.
CUT into small bars.
PLACE bars on a baking sheet.
BAKE on middle oven rack for 10-15 minutes.
LET cool completely.
SPREAD the underside of one-half of the bars with jam. Cover with remaining bars.
PREPARE Chocofix according to package directions. Decorate as desired.

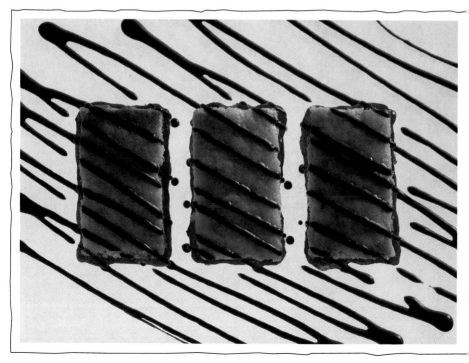

Pine Nut Rectangles

Recipe No. 580

Dough:

300 g	all-purpose flour	2¼	cups
5 mL	**oetker** baking powder	1	tsp
150 g	sugar	⅔	cup
1 pkg	**oetker** vanilla sugar	1	pkg
1	egg yolk	1	
15 mL	milk	1	tbsp
150 g	cold butter or margarine	⅔	cup

Glaze:

1	egg white	1	

Decoration:

55 g	pine nuts	⅓	cup

Dough:

MIX together flour and baking powder.

SIFT onto a working surface.

MAKE a well in the centre. Put sugar, vanilla sugar, egg yolk and milk in the well.

ADD some flour and work into a thick paste.

CUT the cold butter or margarine in small pieces over the flour mixture.

STARTING from the centre, work all ingredients into a smooth dough.

CHILL for one-half hour.

PREHEAT oven to 180°C (350°F).

ROLL out dough thinly.

CUT into 4 x 6 cm (1½ x 2¼") rectangles.

PLACE rectangles on a baking sheet.

USING a fork, beat the egg white.

BRUSH egg white on rectangles. Decorate with pine nuts.

BAKE on middle oven rack for 10-15 minutes.

Coconut Bars

Recipe No. 581

Batter:

250	g	all-purpose flour	1³/₄ cups
1	pkg	**oetker** baking powder	1 pkg
150	g	icing sugar, sifted	1¹/₃ cups
		juice of 1 lemon	
105	mL	coffee	7 tbsp
1		egg	1

Glaze:

250	g	shortening, room temperature	1¹/₄ cups
250	g	icing sugar, sifted	2¹/₄ cups
2	pkgs	**oetker** vanilla sugar	2 pkgs
75	mL	milk	5 tbsp
20	g	cocoa	¹/₄ cup

Decoration:

250	g	coconut, shredded	2¹/₂ cups

Batter:
PREHEAT oven to 180°C (350°F). Grease a 25 x 30 cm (10 x 12") baking sheet. Sprinkle with some flour.
SIFT together flour and baking powder.
MAKE a well in the centre. Put icing sugar, lemon juice, coffee and egg into the well.
STIR for two to three minutes.
SPREAD the batter 1 cm (³/₈") thick on the prepared baking sheet.
BAKE on lower oven rack for 35 minutes.
REMOVE from baking sheet immediately after baking.
COOL completely on a wire rack.
CUT into 1.5 x 4 cm (⁵/₈ x 1¹/₂") bars.

Glaze:
WARM the shortening on low heat.
ADD icing sugar, vanilla sugar, milk and cocoa.
STIR well.
DIP each bar into the glaze. Roll in shredded coconut.

Aniseed Curves

Recipe No. 582

Batter:

4	eggs	4
150 g	icing sugar, sifted	1⅓ cups
1 pkg	**oetker** vanilla sugar	1 pkg
120 g	all-purpose flour	¾ cup

Sprinkling:

some	aniseed	some

Batter:

PREHEAT oven to 180°C (350°F). Grease a baking sheet.

BEAT eggs until fluffy.

GRADUALLY add icing sugar and vanilla sugar.

CONTINUE to beat until mixture is creamy.

SIFT flour over creamed mixture.

FOLD in gently but thoroughly.

USING two teaspoons, scoop out small portions of the mixture and place well apart on prepared baking sheet.

SPRINKLE with aniseed.

BAKE on middle oven rack for 8-10 minutes.

WHILE still hot, bend sheets over a wooden spoon handle.

LET cool.

Glazed Stars

Recipe No. 583

Dough:

235	g	all-purpose flour	1³/₄ cups
15	mL	**oetker** baking powder	1 tbsp
60	g	icing sugar, sifted	¹/₂ cup
1	pkg	**oetker** vanilla sugar	1 pkg
5	drops	**oetker** lemon flavouring concentrate	5 drops
1		egg yolk	1
45	mL	milk	3 tbsp
110	g	cold butter or margarine	¹/₂ cup

Glaze:

250	g	icing sugar	2¹/₄ cups
15	mL	lemon juice	1 tbsp
30	mL	water	2 tbsp

Dough:

MIX together flour and baking powder.
SIFT onto a working surface.
MAKE a well in the centre. Put icing sugar, vanilla sugar, flavouring concentrate, egg yolk and milk into the well.
ADD some flour and work into a thick paste.
CUT the cold butter or margarine in small pieces over the flour mixture.
STARTING from the centre, work all ingredients into a smooth dough.
CHILL for one-half hour.
PREHEAT oven to 180°C (350°F).
ROLL out dough thinly.
USING a star-shaped cookie cutter, cut out stars.
PLACE stars on a baking sheet.
BAKE on middle oven rack for 10-15 minutes.
REMOVE from baking sheet and let cool completely.

Glaze:

SIFT icing sugar into a mixing bowl.
STIR in lemon juice and enough water until mixture is of spreading consistency.
GLAZE stars.

Cheese And Onion Fingers

ecipe No. 584

Dough:

235 g	all-purpose flour	1³/₄	cups
10 mL	**oetker** baking powder	2	tsp
2 mL	salt	¹/₂	tsp
2 mL	paprika	¹/₂	tsp
3	egg yolks	3	
100 g	parmesan cheese, grated	³/₄	cup
15 mL	sour cream	1	tbsp
120 g	almonds, ground	1¹/₃	cups
150 g	cold butter or margarine	²/₃	cup

Filling:

110 g	butter	¹/₂	cup
60 g	parmesan cheese, grated	¹/₂	cup
60 g	Gorgonzola	2¹/₂	oz
some	salt, pepper	some	
2	green onions, thinly sliced	2	

Dough:

MIX together flour and baking powder.
SIFT onto a working surface.
MAKE a well in the centre. Put salt, paprika, egg yolks, parmesan cheese, sour cream and almonds in the well.
ADD some flour and work into a thick paste.
CUT the cold butter or margarine in small pieces over the flour mixture.
STARTING from the centre, work all ingredients into a smooth dough.
CHILL for one-half hour.
PREHEAT oven to 180°C (350°F).
ROLL out dough to a 3 mm (¹/₈") thickness.
CUT into slices 8 cm (3") long and 3 cm (1¹/₄") wide.
PLACE slices on a baking sheet.
BAKE on middle oven rack for 15-20 minutes.
REMOVE from baking sheet. Let cool completely.

Filling:

COMBINE butter, parmesan cheese, Gorgonzola, salt, pepper and green onions.
STIR until mixture is smooth.
SPREAD one-half of the slices with filling. Top with remaining slices.
DECORATE as desired.

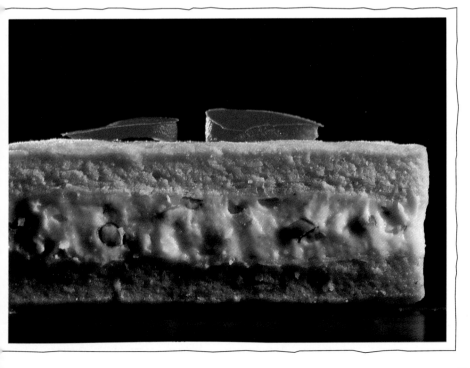

Parmesan Cheese Slices

Recipe No. 585

Dough:

235	g	all-purpose flour	1³/₄	cups
10	mL	**oetker** baking powder	2	tsp
3		egg yolks	3	
1	mL	pepper	¹/₄	tsp
45	mL	sour cream	3	tbsp
170	g	cold butter or margarine	³/₄	cup

Brushing:

1		egg yolk	1	
15	mL	milk	1	tbsp

Sprinkling:

130	g	parmesan cheese, grated	1	cup

Dough:

MIX together flour and baking powder.
SIFT onto a working surface.
MAKE a well in the centre. Put egg yolks, pepper and sour cream in the well.
ADD some flour and work into a thick paste.
CUT the butter or margarine in small pieces over the flour mixture.
STARTING from the centre, work all ingredients into a smooth dough.
CHILL for one-half hour.
PREHEAT oven to 180°C (350°F).
SHAPE dough into 10 cm (4") long sticks, 1.5 cm (⁵/₈") in diameter.
PLACE the sticks on a baking sheet.

Brushing:

WHISK the egg yolk and milk.
BRUSH sticks with egg yolk mixture.
SPRINKLE tops of sticks with parmesan cheese.
BAKE on middle oven rack for 10-15 minutes.

Austrian Charms

Recipe No. 586

Dough:

270 g	all-purpose flour	2	cups
10 mL	**oetker** baking powder	2	tsp
5 mL	salt	1	tsp
1	egg	1	
2	egg yolks	2	
175 g	cold butter or margarine	¾	cup

Brushing:

15 mL	milk	1	tbsp

Sprinkling:

caraway seeds, paprika, poppy seeds

Dough:

MIX together flour and baking powder.

SIFT onto a working surface.

MAKE a well in the centre. Put salt, egg and egg yolks in the well.

ADD flour and work into a thick paste.

CUT the cold butter or margarine in small pieces over the flour mixture.

STARTING from the centre, work all ingredients into a smooth dough.

CHILL for one-half hour.

PREHEAT oven to 180°C (350°F).

ROLL out dough thinly.

USING a variety of cutters, cut out circles, rosettes, squares or heart shapes.

PLACE shapes on a baking sheet.

BRUSH with milk. Sprinkle with caraway or poppy seeds and paprika.

BAKE on middle oven rack for 8-10 minutes.

Desserts

Snow Dumplings with Vanilla Sauce

Recipe No. 587

Ingredients:

3	egg whites	3
100 g	sugar	½ cup

Vanilla Sauce:

1 pkg	**oetker** instant vanilla sauce	1 pkg
250 mL	milk	1 cup

Decoration:

fruit sauce or cranberries
some small chocolate rolls

BEAT egg whites to stiff peaks. (Peaks should be so stiff that when a knife is inserted, the cut remains visible.)

CONTINUE beating. Gradually add the sugar.

FILL a large saucepan with water. Bring to a boil.

USING a spoon, scoop out dumpling-size portions from the egg white mixture.

PLACE in hot water. Simmer for 3-4 minutes on each side.

USING a ladle, remove dumplings from water and drain.

PREPARE vanilla sauce according to package directions.

SERVE sauce as an accompaniment to the dumplings.

DECORATE with fruit sauce, cranberries or chocolate rolls.

Quark-Yoghurt Dumplings with Orange Sauce

Recipe No. 588

Ingredients:

¹/₂ pkg	**oetker** gelatin	¹/₂ pkg	
125 mL	orange juice	¹/₂ cup	
125 mL	lemon juice	¹/₂ cup	
250 g	quark	1 cup	
100 g	icing sugar, sifted	³/₄ cup	
250 mL	yoghurt	1 cup	
375 mL	whipping cream	1¹/₂ cups	

Sauce:

15 mL	**oetker** Gustin corn starch	1 tbsp	
250 mL	orange juice	1 cup	
45 mL	sugar	3 tbsp	
1 pkg	**oetker** vanilla sugar	1 pkg	

Decoration:

some	orange peel	some

Dumplings:

IN a saucepan, dissolve gelatin according to package directions. Add orange and lemon juice. Continue heating until gelatin has completely dissolved.

IN a bowl, combine quark, icing sugar and yoghurt. Stir until smooth.

COMBINE gelatin mixture with a small portion of the quark mixture. Add this to remaining quark mixture. Stir. Let set.

BEAT whipping cream to stiff peaks.

FOLD into partially set quark mixture.

POUR into a bowl and chill for one hour.

Sauce:

COMBINE corn starch with 30 mL (2 tbsp) of the measured orange juice. Stir until smooth.

IN a saucepan, mix together remaining juice, sugar and vanilla sugar. Bring to a boil, while stirring constantly. Gradually add corn starch mixture. Return to a boil.

REMOVE from heat. Let cool. Stir before serving.

SCOOP out dumpling-size portions from the quark mixture. Place in orange sauce. Decorate with peel.

Vanilla Rum Pudding

Recipe No. 589

Ingredients:

1	pkg **oetker** vanilla pudding	1	pkg
30-60	mL sugar	2-4	tbsp
500	mL milk	2	cups
15	mL rum	1	tbsp
1	pkg **oetker** vanilla sugar	1	pkg
125	mL whipping cream	½	cup

Decoration:

red fruits or jam

PREPARE pudding according to package directions.
POUR into a bowl. Cover with plastic wrap and chill.
SHORTLY before serving, beat pudding thoroughly with a whisk.
STIR in rum and vanilla sugar.
BEAT the whipping cream to stiff peaks. (Reserve some whipped cream for decoration.)
SPOON whipped cream over pudding mixture. Fold in gently but thoroughly.
FILL dessert dishes with pudding. Decorate with reserved whipped cream, fruits or jam.

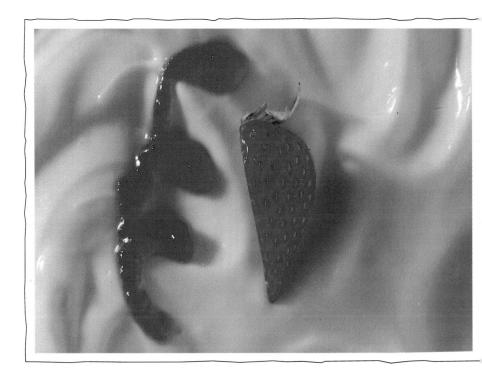

Orange Baskets

Recipe No. 590

Ingredients:

1	pkg	**oetker** vanilla mousse	1 pkg
250	mL	milk	1 cup
4		large oranges	4
1		large apple	1
50	g	hazelnuts, chopped	¹/₂ cup
40	g	pistachio nuts, chopped	¹/₄ cup
30	g	glacé cherries, chopped	¹/₄ cup
1	pkg	**oetker** vanilla sugar	1 pkg
15	mL	rum	1 tbsp

Decoration:

10	mL	**oetker** Whip it	2 tsp
125	mL	whipping cream	¹/₂ cup

PREPARE vanilla mousse according to package directions. Chill.

CUT oranges as illustrated.

REMOVE pulp from the oranges and cut into small pieces.

PEEL, core and cube apple. Add to orange pieces.

MIX in hazelnuts, pistachio nuts and cherries.

SPRINKLE with vanilla sugar.

STIR rum into fruit mixture.

Fold fruit mixture into the mousse.

ADD Whip it to whipping cream and beat until peaks form.

PLACE whipped cream mixture into a pastry bag.

ENSURE orange halves are thoroughly cleaned out.

FILL halves with the fruit mixture. Decorate with whipped cream. (If desired, serve in dessert dishes.)

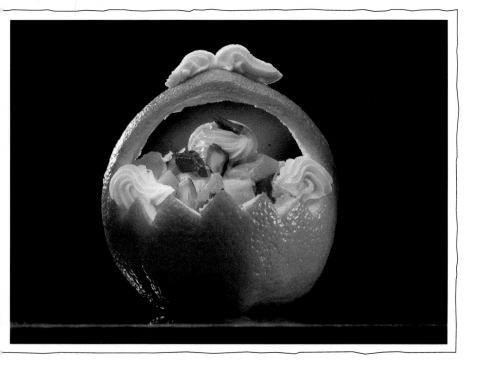

Apple Bundles

Recipe No. 591

Batter:

1	pkg	frozen puff pastry	1 pkg

Filling:

8		medium apples	8
60	mL	raisins	4 tbsp
30	mL	sugar	2 tbsp

Brushing:

1		egg yolk	1
5	mL	milk	1 tsp

THAW puff pastry according to package directions.
PREHEAT oven to 180°C (350°F). Lightly grease a baking sheet.
PEEL and core the apples.
ROLL out dough thinly.
USING a knife, cut out eight squares (depending on the size of the apples).
PLACE an apple in each square.
FILL core of apples with raisins and sugar.
BEAT egg yolk and milk.
BRUSH all four corners of each dough square with the milk mixture.
FOLD all corners of each square over the apples so that corners overlap.
USING a round cookie cutter, cut out circles from remaining dough.
BRUSH circles with milk mixture and press on top of apple. (This will prevent the dough square from slipping.)
BRUSH the dough-covered apples with the remaining milk mixture.
PLACE apples on prepared baking sheet.
BAKE on lower oven rack for 20-25 minutes.

Diamond Pastries

Recipe No. 592

Dough:

270	g	all-purpose flour	2	cups
5	mL	**oetker** baking powder	1	tsp
3		egg yolks	3	
1	pkg	**oetker** vanilla sugar	1	pkg
1	mL	salt	¹/₄	tsp
15	mL	rum	1	tbsp
30-45	mL	sour cream	2-3	tbsp

Deep Frying:

		vegetable oil		

Sprinkling:

40	g	icing sugar	¹/₃	cup
1	pkg	**oetker** vanilla sugar	1	pkg

Dough:

MIX together flour and baking powder.
SIFT onto a working surface.
MAKE a well in the centre. Put egg yolks, vanilla sugar, salt, rum and sour cream in the well.
STARTING from the centre, work all ingredients into a smooth dough.
ROLL out dough. Fold in three.
LET rest for a short time.
REPEAT the rolling and resting three times.
ROLL the dough out very thinly.
USING a knife, cut out slanted rectangles.
FILL a deep fryer half way with vegetable oil.
Heat slowly. During the frying process the temperature should be kept at a constant, 180°C (350°F).
PLACE rectangles into the hot oil. Deep fry until golden brown.
REMOVE from oil with a slotted spoon and drain on paper towels.
PLACE rectangles on wire cooling rack.

Sprinkling:

MIX together icing sugar and vanilla sugar.
SPRINKLE rectangles with sugar mixture.
SERVE with apple sauce or **oetker** instant vanilla sauce.

*O*ld Vienna Apple Strudel

Recipe No. 593

Dough:

235 g	all-purpose flour	1³/₄	cups
15 mL	oil	2	tbsp
2 mL	salt	¹/₂	tsp
125 mL	lukewarm water	¹/₂	cup
	OR		
2 pkgs	Phyllo or strudel dough	2	pkgs

Brushing:

some	butter, melted		some

Sprinkling:

120 g	bread crumbs	1	cup
80 g	butter (second amount)	¹/₃	cup

Filling:

1 kg	cooking apples	2	lbs
	juice and grated peel of		
	1 lemon		
100 g	walnuts, chopped	²/₃	cup
100 g	raisins	²/₃	cup
110 g	sugar	¹/₂	cup
5 mL	cinnamon	1	tsp
1 mL	cloves, ground	¹/₄	tsp
125 mL	whipping cream	¹/₂	cup

Dough:
LIGHTLY grease a baking sheet.
SIFT flour onto a working surface.
MAKE a well in the centre. Put oil, salt and water in the well.
STARTING from the centre work all ingredients into a smooth dough. Knead until dough is blistery. (The longer the dough is kneaded the better it becomes.)
SHAPE dough into a ball. Brush with some melted butter.
PLACE into a warm bowl. Cover. Let rest for one-half hour.
IN a skillet, over medium heat, toast breadcrumbs in butter (second amount) until golden brown.

Apple Filling:
PEEL, core and slice apples thinly.
SPRINKLE with lemon juice.
MIX grated lemon peel, nuts, raisins, sugar, cinnamon and ground cloves.
ADD to apples. Mix well.
BEAT the whipping cream to stiff peaks.
PREHEAT oven to 200°C (400°F).
ROLL the dough out thinly on a kitchen towel sprinkled with flour.
STRETCH the dough by putting it over the back of your hands. Gently pull the dough outwards in all directions. Stretch the dough as thin as possible.
BRUSH the dough with melted butter.
SPRINKLE the toasted breadcrumbs over two-thirds of the dough.
COVER the breadcrumbs with apple filling and top with whipped cream.
FOLD over two sides of the dough using the towel to prevent the filling from escaping.
ROLL up dough tightly (using the towel for help) as you would a jelly-roll, starting at the end with the filling.
PLACE the roll, seam down, on the prepared baking sheet.
BRUSH the roll with the remaining melted butter.
(If the roll is too long, place it on the baking sheet in a crescent shape.)
BAKE on lower oven rack for 35-40 minutes.

Quark Strudel

Dough:

See Apple Strudel

Filling:

500 g	quark	2 cups
2	egg yolks	2
110 g	sugar	¹/₂ cup
1 pkg	**oetker** vanilla sugar	1 pkg
¹/₂ btl	**oetker** lemon flavouring concentrate	¹/₂ btl
¹/₂ pkg	**oetker** vanilla pudding	¹/₂ pkg
100 g	raisins	²/₃ cup
2	egg whites	2

Brushing:

some	butter, melted	some

Filling:

COMBINE quark, egg yolks, two-thirds of the sugar, vanilla sugar, flavouring concentrate and pudding.

BEAT until fluffy.

FOLD in raisins gently but thoroughly.

BEAT egg whites to stiff peaks.

CONTINUE to beat. Gradually add the remaining sugar.

FOLD egg white mixture into quark mixture gently but thoroughly.

BRUSH the "pulled" dough with some melted butter.

COVER one-half of the dough with the cheese filling.

FOLD over two sides of the dough using the towel to prevent the filling from escaping.

ROLL up the dough tightly, as you would a jelly roll, starting from the end with the filling.

PLACE the roll, seam down, onto the prepared baking sheet.

BRUSH the roll with the remaining melted butter.

BAKE on lower oven rack for 35-40 minutes.

Recipe Index

Personal Notes

The oetker *Library of Baking*

Baking is Fun — The ABC's of Baking This book will guide you through a variety of baking techniques. Learn how to prepare batters, doughs, fillings and glazes. Complete with decorating ideas and helpful hints.

Baking Is Fun — Volume 1 (Recipe No. 1 - 93) Prepare Traditional European desserts such as Black Forest Cake, Hazelnut Cream Torte and Apple Strudel with the aid of this book.

Baking Is Fun — Volume 2 (Recipe No. 94 - 190) A unique collection of European baking specialties.

Baking Is Fun — Volume 3 (Recipe No. 191 - 270) This volume consists of Traditional Holiday recipes for the Christmas season. This volume also contains a special section on recipes for diabetics.

Baking Is Fun — Volume 4 (Recipe No. 271 - 350) Light Wholesome Baking is the principal theme of Volume 4. Make a soufflé, a specialty bread or a gourmet dessert. There are many recipes to choose from.

Baking Is Fun — Volume 5 (Recipe No. 351 - 433) This volume contains a rich assortment of tempting yeast recipes.

Baking Is Fun — Volume 6 (Recipe No. 434 - 513) This volume, entitled "Specialties of the World", takes you on a culinary trip around the world with recipes from Austria to Australia and China to Sicily.

Baking Is Fun — Volume 7 (Recipe No. 514 - 593) Our newest addition to the Baking Is Fun library. This volume contains many Classic European recipes.

To order these books please write to:

oetker Recipe Service
2229 Drew Road
Mississauga, Ontario
L5S 1E5